RAY MEARS
NORTHERN WILDERNESS

HODDER

First published in Great Britain in 2009 by Hodder & Stoughton
An Hachette UK company

First published in paperback in 2010

2

Copyright © Ray Mears 2010

By arrangement with the BBC

A CIP catalogue record for this title is available from the British Library.

ISBN 978 0 340 98083 5

Printed and bound in the UK by Clays Ltd, St Ives plc

Hodder & Stoughton policy is to use papers that are natural,
renewable and recyclable products and made from wood
grown in sustainable forests. The logging and manufacturing
processes are expected to conform to the environmental
regulations of the country of origin.

Hodder & Stoughton Ltd
338 Euston Road
London NW1 3BH

www.hodder.co.uk

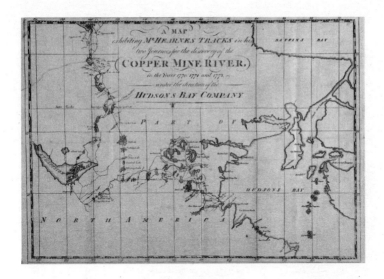

CONTENTS

INTRODUCTION

There are places on earth that are so vast, they still impress upon us the power of nature, and Canada is full of them. This book complements the journey I made in filming a television series – a voyage across the magnificent northern wilderness and back into history. It's a history written by explorers who should be household names in their native Britain, but who are now as little known as the land they encountered.

I had been very much looking forward to this adventure. The northern wilderness is a place I've truly come to love. It's a place where knowledge and experience are still far more important than the equipment you carry with you.

There is a seemingly endless list of superlatives that

springs to mind when talking about Canada – a vast country that sprawls over almost 10 million square kilometres, making it the second-largest in the world after Russia. With over two million lakes, Canada is host to about a tenth of the world's fresh water, and embraces the longest coastline of any country. It's also the location of the largest land biome on the planet. There's a vastness to this country that is almost unimaginable in its scale – an epic grandeur in its landscapes, its forests, rivers, ice and snow, its mountains, wildlife and wilderness. This is a stunning, varied, challenging and dramatic land that is breathtakingly beautiful, and still largely unspoilt.

No matter how many times I travel there, I'm always staggered by the sheer scale of this country; in fact, it almost defies cerebral comprehension. Perhaps the most stunning statistic of all is that my homeland, the United Kingdom, would fit comfortably within its borders 40 times over. That's how differently you have to think about distance here – everything is so very much larger, and so unbelievably spread out.

This is a land known for the fierceness of its winters. The city of Yellowknife, in the Northwest Territories, is so cold that the average night-time temperature in the months of December, January and February is minus 30 degrees Celsius. In the province of Manitoba, the city of Thompson – with a population about 13,500 – is so cold that it is only frost-free for about two months of the year.

Every part of the country has a different story to tell. I could travel to the badlands of the province of Alberta, where the fossil records of dinosaurs are in such abundance that the area has been proclaimed a UNESCO World Heritage Site. Or I could paddle down the length of the Mackenzie River – a 4,241-kilometre journey from the Great Slave Lake to the edge of the Arctic Ocean. If, instead, I turned south-east from the lake, I would enter the territory that established one of the greatest companies the world has ever seen – the Hudson's Bay Company – where a Royal Charter, enacted only four years after the Great Fire of London, created a company that was, at one time, the largest landowner in the world. Canada's history is rich and varied, and firmly woven into the tapestry of the landscape and the people who live here.

But that's not why I love this country. I love coming here because the history of the nation is firmly entwined with the land, and with the ways in which the land was opened up and explored. It's a country that it took a woodsman's skills to explore, and bushcraft knowledge to survive. The first European explorers of Canada came to the country and revealed its treasures to the world, establishing its borders and mapping its wild interior. But they were only able to achieve all of these things thanks to the skills they learned from the First Nations – people who had lived for centuries in harmony with what can be one of the harshest environments on the planet.

The men who made extraordinary journeys across the land, such as the unnamed Frenchmen who followed French navigator Jacques Cartier up unexplored rivers and across vast lakes in search of the valuable beaver pelts, may now be largely forgotten, but their compatriots have their names – in some cases literally – carved into the landscape. These include explorers and fur traders Pierre-Esprit Radisson and Médard Chouart des Groseilliers, who accelerated the growth of the fur trade when they took their expansionist plans to King Charles II's court; David Thompson; Sir Alexander Mackenzie; Dr John Rae; and, the greatest of them all, Samuel Hearne. I have followed in the footsteps of some of these great men, to demonstrate what they suffered and learned as they walked, sometimes alone, into the deep woods, into a place that demanded that they adopt the ways of the land and the people who lived there. Canada is a country whose borders owe their very existence to the skills of those intrepid and largely unsung heroes. I wanted to use not only my own bushcraft skills but theirs as well as I travelled around what is, for me, one of the greatest places I know. As far as I'm concerned, there is no wilderness on earth that can ever match this northern wilderness.

CHAPTER 1

THE FORGOTTEN FOREST

The heart of this natural world, the heart of this northern wilderness is the extraordinary boreal forest. This is land that held no interest for Europeans until the 18th century. The harsh climate, short growing season, and apparent lack of natural resources, such as gold and other precious commodities that might make them rich, led explorers from Europe to believe that this was land that was not worth investigating or settling. They had no idea of the natural 'riches' that did exist in the depths of this beautiful hinterland. For thousands of years the First Nations had been living here in partnership with the natural world – never trying to subdue it, but living from its bounty in safety and comfort.

The expanse of the boreal forest is overwhelming. One-third of Canada is carpeted with a mosaic of trees and water, a rich and unique mixture of trees flourishing in the harshest of environments. A dynamic system of living organisms, plants, animals, insects and micro-organisms, interacting with the physical environment of soil, water and air, the boreal forest is an inter-connected web of life that calls to me deeply. It's a place I love and long to explore. To understand Canada, you have to understand this forest.

Its name is taken from the Greek god *Boreas*, the god of the northern wind. If you think of the term *Aurora Borealis* – the Northern Lights – you'll get an idea of the provenance of the name. The boreal forest is, to my mind, probably the most under-rated environment on the planet. It sits on the shoulders of Canada like a cloak, and stretches in a band that is almost 1,000 kilometres wide, and runs more than 5,000 kilometres from the Yukon in the West to Newfoundland on the Atlantic coast. If you were in space, looking down on the Earth, you'd see that it carries on through Alaska and across the top of Russia, through Finland, Sweden and Norway, and

even clips the north of Scotland on its way to forming a massive trans-continental forest. The boreal forest is one of the largest in the world, with the Canadian territories making up a quarter of what is a vast green crown bigger than the Amazon jungle, and totalling one-third of the world's entire forest system. It's one of the largest biomes on earth, but it is still, inexplicably, virtually unheard of.

The forest was formed over 10,000 years ago, when the ice sheets retreated, but I doubt that it's changed very much in all the centuries since then. One of the distinguishing features of the forest is its uniformity; the natural disturbances it faces – fire, or plagues of beetles or other insects that can kill the trees – occur in a cyclical way, thus ensuring that every 75 to 100 years the forest is renewed. Since European immigration to the continent, man's efforts to fight the fires have altered this balance, but nature still makes light work of the constant regeneration that keeps this forest alive and thriving. So, too, the wildlife and the native people live their lives according to, and are dependent upon, the cycles of the boreal forest.

The well-established coastal species of trees found further south have no place here; this is a land dominated by the coniferous pine, spruce and fir, deciduous birch and, in the southern reaches of the forest, poplar and aspen trees – all of them sitting on a deep, spongy mass of lichens, moss and peat.

The peat area towards the northern boundaries of the forest incorporates the world's largest store of organic carbon, and, through the packed soil, millions upon millions of litres of water are filtered daily; indeed, the trees and these peatlands comprise one of the world's largest carbon reservoirs. Under the closed cover of the forest, away from the peat areas, things are different. The limited light and air movement down at ground level reduces the complexity of the habitat and the variety of plant life, while the needle litter is not only slow to decompose, but also helps to maintain the soil's acidity.

Along with elk, moose, black bears, lynx, coyotes, foxes and wolves, the forest provides a temporary home to half of all North America's birds, with estimates of the numbers of birds that migrate north to breed in the boreal forest every year varying between 1.65 to 3 billion. In fact, some even put the number as high as 5 billion.

HUNTER-GATHERERS

And it's not just the birds and the animals that are drawn to live here. Before the Europeans arrived, this land was inhabited by nomadic hunter-gatherers, living off everything that the forest provided. Canada was home to many different First Nation people – the Huron, Algonquin,

Chippewa and Ojibwa, to name but a few. Inexplicably, however, in the history of North America, the people of the forest have tended to be sidelined, overlooked in favour of the plains Indians further south. My feeling is that the people who lived here were less visible in history because the forest would not support large gatherings; resources were scarce and spread out, so the people of this sprawling forest needed to live some distance apart from each other. Nonetheless, this was a reliable and plentiful home for those who understood the world around them in a way we'll never fully comprehend.

Those First Nations communities numbered over a million strong, a figure that means little against the vast backdrop of the forest. These were people who chose to spend their lives in the forest, rather than 'on the ground' – the term used by elders to describe life outside its boundaries. Their way of life was dependent upon the forest, so they took from it only what could easily be replenished. Theirs was a sustainable lifestyle because they did not have the technology that would create a greater impact on its

renewable resources. The forest provided bark and pitch for canoes, as well as wood for fuel; the animals they hunted gave them meat and skins for clothing. But it wasn't a basic life. Clothing was embroidered with moose hair, porcupine quills were worked into floral and geometric designs, eating bowls were carved from spruce, and their dwellings were created from spruce with intricate birch bark coverings.

If you want to find out more, I recommend David Henry's

book *Canada's Boreal Forest*. He is a convervation ecologist and author, who has been studying the boreal forest for much of his life, and has become a world-renowned expert on it. He has devoted a good part of his career to challenging the perception of the boreal forest as an economic wasteland, drawing attention to how economically and ecologically valuable it is. David travelled with me on part of my journey to share my appreciation of the forest.

One of the places I visited was Beaver Lodge, an isolated cabin on the shores of Asawaan Lake in Prince Albert National Park. This was home to an extraordinary man, born in Hastings in England in 1888 under the name Archibald Belaney. He was passionate about animals and an early conservationist who emigrated to live in this remote spot. He wore long braids and buckskin and took the name Grey Owl, in imitation of the First Nations people he so admired, and he tried to protect the animals in his vicinity, particularly from the cruelty of animal traps. I very much enjoyed seeing his remote cabin, which remains much as he left it on his death in 1938.

I prefer to explore the boreal forest in the autumn, when the mosquito population has died right back. Of the plethora of wildlife that inhabits this forest, my indisputable favourite creature to study is the beaver. Without these animals, with their sharp front teeth, the forest would not only lose its character but its very existence would be challenged. The beaver has made Canada the country we know today.

THE BEAVER

Without the beaver, I'd find the fundamental act of getting around the forest very difficult. Canoeing is sometimes the only way to get about, as there are few roads or even passable paths within the forest. Thanks to the activities of the beaver, large sections of the rivers that thread their way through the forest are held back by dams, and these not only keep the rivers upstream from the dams in plenty of water, but also provide a habitat for abundant fish – adding to the diversity of the forest by providing food for hungry predators.

Beavers are fascinating creatures to spend time with. I've canoed right up to a beaver's lodge, and it was huge. It had been created over the summer months by a family of beavers, and inside were chambers where they could feed and sleep safely. The dam was built so that the water level was high enough to ensure that the only way into their mound was underwater – thus providing the beavers with the security they need.

When I was there, in autumn, the beavers were just completing the mound, covering it in mud, which would freeze in the winter to create a solid cap to protect them from predators burrowing in, and offering a more solid insulating layer. Snow falls on top of this, keeping the temperature of the lodge warm enough to sustain the beavers throughout the winter.

That's one thing I learned on my travels throughout this northern wilderness – snow is an excellent insulator, comprised of about 90 per cent air. The millions of air pockets trap the heat beneath its surface. One test showed that the temperature near the ground, under several feet of snow, was about 10 degrees Celsius warmer than in the air above, and this temperature is maintained throughout the cold winter months, thus ensuring the survival of small mammals such as rodents who make their homes under the snow. Beavers, too, make use of the excellent insulating properties of snow, and ensure that their lodges are firm, broad and flat enough to sustain several feet of snow in winter.

Because the beavers are nocturnal, these lodges just seem to appear in the landscape. It's easy to understand why early Europeans thought the beavers were more like human builders because of the ingenuity they showed. Their dams and lodges are feats of engineering that are incredible in their breadth and careful planning.

Beavers do not hibernate in winter. They brave the cold waters under the ice to swim to their rafts, structures on which they store food, which are normally situated several metres away from the lodge. They are able to survive in the icy waters thanks to an unusual metabolic tactic. Before leaving the safety of their chambers they elevate their body temperature slightly, which gives them a few more minutes in the water before their body temperature drops too far.

They're pretty sturdy animals, too, growing to over 1.2 metres in length, and weighing over 26 kilograms. They can fell a native balsam poplar, with a diameter of 25 centimetres, within four to five hours. The animal will turn its head sideways and chew into the wood, slicing chunks out by biting at the top and the bottom of the chosen area, and then ripping it out from the middle.

The beaver has to sharpen its teeth every 15 minutes or so, but this is undertaken naturally by the action of chewing through wood. The front of the beaver's tooth is hardened with enamel but the back of the tooth is made of softer dentine, and, as the beaver chews, the softer material wears away, allowing the sharp edge to be restored.

The beaver's aim in gnawing down trees is to collect the younger bark on the topmost branches, on which it feeds. They have to take down a number of trees to make sure they have enough bark to get them through the winter. None of the tree is wasted, however; the trunks are dragged to bridge streams, creating ponds and redirecting the water flow. Branches are used to create their ingenious lodges and food rafts.

Beavers are the engineers of the boreal forest. More than just builders, they modify the whole landscape around their lodge, creating watery channels off into the woods around their home by felling trees and dragging them back. The forest itself is changed by their behaviour, and they play a vital role in maintaining the habitat in which they and every other animal lives. In the next chapter, we'll learn just why beavers played such a pivotal role in the history of Canada.

MUSKEG

Everything in the woods around me contributes to the sustainability of the forest and the wildlife and people who live here. That's an important fact to understand. The boreal forest isn't just a static landscape – it's a living entity, a collective where everything plays its part. Because of its size, it isn't always possible to see the wildlife in the boreal forest, astherearesomanyplacestomoveontointhesearchforfood,or to take shelter, but you can always spot the signs that animals have been there.

If you're going to be moving about in the woods, or even staying out overnight, then it is a very good idea to know what might be lurking so you can protect yourself from anything that might take an interest in you. Armed with this knowledge, you can enter the true spirit of the woods. And that spirit is literally all around you.

Autumn is an interesting time to walk through the woods, as they are littered with the materials that many animals are preparing to store away for the long cold winter ahead. Walking the trail, I found a mushroom at the top of a small shrub, where it had been placed to dry by a red squirrel. If he remembered where he'd put it, he would come back to collect his dehydrated mushroom and take it up into the trees to stash away in his winter larder. Another sign that there are squirrels about are the half-chewed buds of jack pine cones lying on the forest floor. Squirrels busily chew off the buds and, when they are ready, they collect the greener ones and store them away. The more mature cones may be eaten on the spot.

The activities of squirrels, in particular, have traditionally acted as a sign to locals that the temperature has reached minus 30 degrees Celsius, the exact point at which the squirrel burrows underground. So if it's freezing outside and you don't see any squirrels about, you'll know that it's cold enough to drive them under.

A large part of the boreal forest's ground is covered with a fine-feathered sphagnum moss, and this area is named 'muskeg' – a Chippewa word meaning 'grassy bog'. The bog forms in areas where the winters are wet and the summers cool, and where the permafrost doesn't allow the excess water to sink down through the soil. Instead, it collects near the surface, making the top level spongy and, in places, dangerous. The 'soil' can give way under heavy weight if the ground underneath is sodden enough, and large moose, for example, can sink into boggy pits if they are unwary. In 1870, in Northern Ontario, a railway engine was 'swallowed' by the ground when the track was laid directly onto muskeg.

The waterlogged ground of the boreal forest provides a perfect nursery for sphagnum moss. This moss was used by the First Nations as a wound dressing and even as nappies for babies. It's not only extremely absorbent – taking up to 750 times its own weight in water – but its natural acidity makes it antiseptic, thus preventing many bacterial infections. Dried, it makes an excellent insulating material.

Walking through the woods with David Henry, I noticed many types of sphagnum, and learned that there are 17 different species in this part of the forest (we have less than a handful in the UK). David pointed out its central importance in the boreal forest.

'It's an ancient plant,' he said. 'We have fossils [of sphagnum moss] going back 90 million years and it looks very much the same. And, yet, it determines what trees, what shrubs grow on this site.'

The same acidity that makes it beneficial for dressing

wounds means that only acid-tolerant plants can grow where it covers the ground. Under the cool, acid conditions of the Northern boreal forest, dead sphagnum moss does not decay but forms a layer of peat. Peat and dissolved salts form a hardpan, preventing water from draining into the underground aquifers of permeable rock. The thick covering of moss also lowers the nutrients in the area and prevents decomposition, so the peat moss starts to raise itself up in layers, creating a soft, damp cover.

'It's one of the dominant plants in the boreal forest, yet it's only half the size of my thumb,' said David.

It's also very beautiful – its rich red colouring provides a vivid contrast against the greens and browns around it. But you have to get down on its level to really see its intricacies and appreciate its microscopic perfection. From above, it forms a magnificent carpet, firmly controlling what plants can join it in its acid, nutrient-poor environment, and playing an important role in reducing the world's carbon footprint.

LOOKING UPWARDS

Looking down, you'll see plenty of evidence of life in the forest — stores of food, half-eaten plants and animals, footprints, traces of feathers and fur, and even scat (animal droppings). But looking upwards at the trees themselves will provide you with even greater proof of the multifarious wildlife that makes the boreal forest its home.

Five-toed claw marks in the bark will tell you that bears have been there. The mother black bear teaches her cubs to climb trees in order to stay out of reach of predators or any other kind of threat. It's possible to tell from the spacing of the claw marks how recent they are. As the tree ages, so the bark grows and spreads, taking the markings with it, so the more widely spaced markings are older.

Rows of nice little holes set in horizontal lines in the bark will indicate that there is a member of the woodpecker family about. The red-breasted sapsucker taps into the bark to create little reservoirs into which sap will flow, and the bird will come along later and harvest the sugary syrup. A larger hole I found, just above ground level, was made by a pileated woodpecker, a spectacular and surprisingly large bird – almost the size of a crow, but with a splendid red crest. They make holes in tree trunks to allow them access to the ants' nests inside. Sometimes the holes they make are large enough to cause the tree to snap in two.

Trees are, of course, a central part of the living fabric of the forest. For example, the leaves of the balsam fir provide

shelter and a constant source of food for moose in the winter. The First Nations used to open the little blisters that grow all over the bark and squeeze out the resin inside, which they would use to treat cuts and even burns. They've done so for centuries. It's a simple but effective form of bush medicine that has undoubtedly stood the test of time.

The people living in the forests in the times before the white explorers ventured into them had acquired skills and knowledge that would help to ensure their survival; there are no records, for example, of scurvy among the First Nations people. How was this possible in a diet that was so restricted, even in the height of summer?

One source of vitamin C was a low-lying evergreen shrub called the Labrador plant, a member of the Heath family. It has strongly aromatic leaves, which can be used to make a palatable herbal tea (although it's toxic if you drink too much), and edible berries. Both leaves and berries are rich in vitamin C that would stave off scurvy and help to keep the First Nations people healthy. Berries that they didn't or couldn't eat were used as dyes for clothing. There was and is little waste in the forest; everything is carefully harvested to ensure that it remains sustainable.

The tamarack larch tree is a staple feature of the boreal forest, albeit a very slow-growing one. David showed me the rings inside one he'd cut down and, while the trunk fitted comfortably in the palm of my hand, I was amazed to learn that it was over 100 years old. The rings fitted together so tightly that I had to use the magnification on my binoculars to be able to distinguish between those at the centre of the trunk. On our travels, David told me that the slender trees growing closely together in one thicket were probably not less than 150 years old, although they looked no more than a few decades old in comparison to the European larches with which we're more familiar.

The tamarack is a resilient and particularly useful tree in the region; it was a favourite of the forest inhabitants, and used for making snowshoes, toboggans (required for carrying loads when the land was covered with snow) and, significantly, tent poles, as the wood is supple and will bend into shape more easily than some of the other hard woods in the area. Tamarack is loaded with oils, which is why it's so flexible. It also had other traditional uses; for example, the softer, inner lining of the bark would be stripped from the tree and used as a poultice to treat cuts and frostbite. Tamarack's hardiness means that it can withstand the severe temperatures that characterise winter in the northern wilderness; however, as you travel northwards, the height of the trees declines, in some parts reaching no more than a quarter of the height they would attain further south.

Also native to the area is the stunning paper birch tree, known as the 'Lady of the Northern Forests'. It grows to heights of over 15 metres, and its leaves turn a glorious golden yellow in the autumn, contrasting beautifully with its silvery-white bark. The bark is partly responsible for the survival of the moose during the winter months; although nutritionally poor, it is abundant and provides sustenance until spring arrives. The paper birch is also an excellent fuel – and I can testify to how well it burns through personal experience. Over the years I have spent many a night in the forest, and the heat produced by my paper-birch fire has always sustained me well.

OVERNIGHT IN THE WOODS

I rely on the traditional skills of woodsmen to navigate and survive this untamed wilderness. You shouldn't venture out without first learning how to stay safe and secure overnight, because if you step off the trail to have a closer look at some of the eye-catching species of plants and animals, you can lose your path within a few paces. Stick to the trails, and you'll easily find your way out again. There are a few other simple tips to bear in mind to ensure that you appreciate rather than fear the boreal forest. It's perfectly possibly to be comfortable here – day or night.

If you find yourself lost, the first thing to do is to stop. Put down your pack, have a drink, and look around you. Think about where you are, and whether you've got something around you that will help you to get back on the path. Are there broken branches or trampled plants showing your route? If it's cold, have something to eat or drink. If you are dehydrated or your body temperature has fallen, your brain will, more often than not, work better once you've had something to drink or a little food. Everything may suddenly become clear.

If not, then you need to establish your position a little better. Find a fixed position from which to work: where better than the place where you first discover you are lost? This is likely to be the nearest point to where you will be found, as well. Old-timers will take some moss from the ground and place it high up in a tree, where it doesn't grow naturally. This provides a good visual marker to help you track your path. I carry high-visibility marker tape, which I'll tie off at about eye-level across some branches and young trees when I leave the path, so that I am always sure where I've come from. When I'm lost, I do the same, to help me chart my search for a route back to the path. Look around for something that you might recognise from your trip into the forest, always keeping in visual contact with your markers.

It's common for people to get lost towards the end of the day, when the light fades and exhaustion sets in. It's probably a bad idea to attempt bushwhacking in the dark, as you'll only become more lost, and probably begin to panic, too. A much better idea is to calm down and accept the idea that you are better off staying where you are for the night. In the morning, when you've got daylight on your side, you'll be able to solve the problem and get going again. For now, however, you'll need a shelter for the night.

Take your time, and stay calm. Don't rush things, which can cause you to build up a sweat; this will wet your clothing and make you even colder, particularly as night falls. Find a space where it's possible to lie down, and where there is already some natural shelter, such as low-hanging branches or some sturdy tree trunks. I built a shelter in the boreal wood by leaning pieces of dead wood against a tree that had fallen down. I didn't break any living branches from trees.

Even if it's not raining, a temporary shelter can be psychologically reassuring. If rain is on the cards, just pile on even more dead wood; you'd be amazed at just how well it works to keep out the cold and the elements, if you layer it on the outside of a shelter. Choose your wood carefully. The smell of the spruce, for example, usefully wards off some of the insects that would otherwise plague you.

I took a thick stick and scraped at the ground in front of my shelter, digging out a shallow trench by lifting away the grass and moss, and rolling back the matted turf. I didn't want to leave much mess behind me – after all, it wasn't the forest's fault I had wandered off the path and decided to stay the night there. The trench was long enough to run the full length of my shelter, and support a long trunk from a fallen paper birch tree, which would burn well into the night and provide me with heat from my head to my toes. This would be vital if the temperature dipped overnight. As it was, I wasn't particularly worried about keeping warm. It was still autumn, and the extreme cold of the winter months had not yet set in. Even if it had been earlier in the season, I'd still have made the fire – not just to provide a little psychological comfort, but also to help keep the bugs away.

I started the fire by building a small platform of dry sticks and then placed birch bark kindling and some small branches on top. The great advantage of using long logs is that they are an efficient way to heat the whole of a shelter without having to stoke the fire too often. Because the wood in the north is quite low in moisture, it's possible to use it fairly soon after it has fallen from the tree.

With my fire underway, I returned to my shelter and removed any branches sticking out of the trunk that might cause me to trip or become injured in the dark. I laid out my bedding and I was ready. I could curl up there, with my fire in front of me, and that was all I needed to see the night through. You don't need a lot of space in your shelter – just enough to curl up in.

Once you've committed to staying in a shelter for the night, you can prepare to get some rest and be ready in the morning to set about finding your way out of the forest again. You've taken a positive step towards solving your problem, and all of a sudden psychology is in your favour.

In the boreal forest, it's always a good idea to bring a pair of gloves and a head-net to keep the insects off. If I'd been travelling in bug season, my overnight stay outdoors would have been vastly improved by these simple items. The insect population of the boreal forest is vast, and the biting insects – mosquitoes, black flies, midges and horse flies – are, the Entomological Society of Canada helpfully says, 'especially numerous in the boreal zone'. As they should be – it's estimated that there are over 33,000 species of insect in the boreal forest area alone, and that's the low end of the estimate.

INSECTS AND MAMMALS

Insects perform the essential function of pollinating many of the plants in the forest, and they are also a valuable food source for the millions of birds that migrate through the area. Try to remember that when they're swarming around you. They can make a simple trek through the woods pretty unbearable if you're not properly covered and prepared to deal with them.

The original inhabitants of the forest used locally available repellents to keep the insects away. They would try anything, from using extracts from plants such as bloodroot – a small plant whose white flowers carpet the ground in the spring – and bay leaves, to smearing animal fat and fish oil on their skin. Some methods were more effective than others; for instance, the sap of the bloodroot plant can be toxic to humans, even though deer can happily feast on it in the spring.

There are so many insects in the forest and so few nutrients available that some plants have evolved to use insects as food. Pitcher plants capture their prey in hollow stalks from which the insects cannot escape, while sundews have sticky threads growing on their leaves to trap and draw in the insects.

Elk, moose, caribou, deer and other large mammals, while not as numerous as the insect life, are plentiful enough to supply the needs of the forest's human inhabitants. The flesh, skins and fur of the large animals, such as the elk, were a crucial resource to the First Nations. The best time to hunt them was probably when the young animals were maturing in the autumnal months, when the cow elks were no longer needed for their survival. Cow elks would be surrounded by bull elks – with their magnificent antlers – once they'd given birth and were ready to rut again. But hunting elk was not a straightforward process; their markings and the muted shades on their fur make for very effective camouflage and help them blend in beautifully with the forest so it took a skilled huntsmen to bring one down.

It's these larger mammals – the elk, the caribou and the moose – that sustained the way of life of the people of the forest. Their skins were used for clothing and shelter, which would be produced by the women in the camps. The men went out and hunted these larger beasts, safe in the knowledge that the women were at home stoking the home fires. This wasn't just division of labour, this was complete interdependence – human life reflecting the life of the forest. A man without a woman to provide his clothing was as good as dead in a place like this. Similarly a woman might have been able to trap small game, but it was moose and caribou that kept her and her way of life alive and she relied on the men to provide them.

The smaller mammals, such as squirrels and the snowshoe hare, are ever-present in the forest. David Henry and I went to look at a squirrels' midden, where they carefully store their food supplies in advance of the grim winters. Outside their burrows we came across heaps of black spruce and jack pine cones, which they would take into the interior of the midden and bury. The mound that we visited had been there, said David, for 30 years; it was partly manufactured from the shells of the cones that had been discarded, so the squirrels could take the seeds inside.

The snowshoe hare is another important part of life in the forest but, unlike the squirrel, it chooses not to hibernate in the cold weather. Instead, its fur changes colour from brown to white, giving it a considerable degree of protection against hunters. However, the presence of the hares means that there is always the chance of finding food for the large predators in the boreal forest, even when the weather is at its harshest. The hares are hunted by lynx, wolves, coyotes and owls, and their population surges and dwindles in relation to the number of predators about.

Interestingly, nature implements her own form of population control, by making the tender shoots of some of the low-lying plants on which hares feed toxic when the plants have been browsed too heavily. This results in a massive reduction in the number of snowshoe hares, which is essential because they could upset the balance in the forest if they became too plentiful.

In autumn, and when I returned to the forest again in winter, I saw animals that I had only read about in books. In the winter months, the snow provided an excellent means of tracking them. Unusually, all three main canines – wolves, foxes and coyotes – co-exist here in yet another example of perfectly balanced nature. The wolves are pack hunters, and go for the larger prey, such as elk. Foxes feed on the rodents and smaller mammals, while coyotes can adapt to either way of hunting – becoming a sort of middleman that hunts in packs occasionally, or a solitary hunter who makes the most of the smaller prey.

WILD RICE

It isn't always harsh in the boreal forest. When the summer months arrive, plenty of produce is available to harvest and store for winter. In particular, in the lakes and by the edge of rivers grows wild rice (brought to the boreal forest from lakes further south). Wild rice is a high-protein grain, rich in vitamins and minerals, and one of the most important foods harvested by the First Nations. An early Ojibway name for wild rice was *Manitou gi ti gahn*, which means 'the plant the Great Spirit gave us'. That name has now been shortened to *manoomin* (derived from *min*, meaning seed and *Minido*, the name for the providing spirit).

Traditionally, during late August and early September, Ojibwa people gathered for the harvest in family groups along the shores of wild rice lakes. It was a time of camaraderie, hard work and offerings of thanks to the spirit-givers. Harvesting was by birch bark canoe. Sticks were used to bend and tap the wild rice plants, making ripe hulls fall into the canoe. The plentiful supplies of rice ensured that there was abundant food for the winter months, and it was a staple in the First Nations diet.

I went out to gather the rice with Tom Charles, who works for Northern Lights Foods. We used a canoe to paddle into the high grasses by the side of the waterways, and Tom pulled the grass over into the canoe, using one hand, with a stick resting in his palm, so that the head of the grass was over a collecting sheet he'd spread out. He beat this stick with another stick held in his other hand. The stick rather than the grass was tapped, leaving the stalk itself safe. The seeds start ripening from the top of the grass downwards, so only tapping the grass from the top ensured that Tom released the more mature seeds, and he could keep coming back to harvest the seeds four or five times each summer. It also meant there were enough seeds on the stalk to ensure growth for next year.

Nowadays there is a more modern method of harvesting. Northern Lights Foods harvests the wild rice by sending out large flat-bottomed boats to cruise slowly through the rice fields, at about 15 kilometres per hour, with scoops affixed to the front to lift the rice off the plants. Tom told me that they often pick up ducks this way, too. It's one way to ensure that the forest can be sustained and yet also economically productive – something crucially important to the people who want to protect its status. Using this method of harvest means a lot of grain drops back into the lake. It's not wasted, as the grain seeds itself and grows back for next year's crop, but it lacks the focused approach of the traditional method. The traditional harvesting technique is slow but I must say there was something very peaceful about paddling along in Tom's canoe.

To prepare the rice, first of all Tom had to parch it by stirring it continuously over the heat with a tiny amount of water – enough to steam it, but without bringing it to the boil. This ensures that the kernel inside the grain hardens up, Tom explained to me, which prevents it from becoming starchy. He moved it around to prevent it from burning until the husk separated from the grains and they started to turn black. Then they are boiled for 40 minutes, with a couple of changes of water, and at last they were ready to eat. And the wild rice was delicious; the flavour of the grain was exceptional – much stronger and tastier than ordinary rice, and with a great texture.

'It's a seasonal job,' Tom told me, talking about the rice harvest, 'and there are maybe 1,400 to 1,500 people doing it. We enjoy the bush; we respect the bush. There's not much to say about it; people just have to go out and experience it.'

About half a kilogram of rice that he collects in the lakes and waterways becomes about two kilograms once it has been cooked, as it expands in the process. Although its harvest is a time-consuming operation, the rice remains a staple for native communities, and has significant cultural, religious and even economic importance.

WATER AND FIRE

It's surprising that in a land where water is so abundant, the forest is entirely dependent upon fire. The interdependence between the growth cycles of the forest and the fires that rampage through them is not yet fully understood, and it is something that has been the focus of much intensive study.

Conservationist David Henry brought along some jack pine cones to show me how this relationship works.

'There are so many things here that have adapted to

life in the northern woods, but the jack pine comes in first place,' he said.

The cones are not particularly big – no more than five centimetres or so long – and they are tightly closed, almost smooth. They are called 'serotinous' – that is, the cones are held tightly together by resins, which only melt in the heat of fires. And so it is only in those fires that the seeds inside the cones are released to allow new life to germinate. As the cones can stay on the tree for 20 years, it means that when fire strikes, they're high enough in the air for the seeds to drift slowly down to the ground when the heat's died down. Or, if there's a breeze, they can move through the warm air, keeping away from the flames below, to settle elsewhere. After 20 years, the seeds inside the cones are as fresh and as able to germinate as they would be in much younger cones.

The relationship between fire and the regeneration of the tree population wasn't written about till the 1970s, so it's a relatively new theory. To test it, I built a fire by the riverbank to see how it affected the jack pine cones. Sure enough, after I placed the branch over a fire, the cone opened up like a flower coming into bloom. The heat of the fire also released the pitch, which fuelled the flames enough to assist the process, and I could soon see the dormant seeds inside. There was a layer of cork nestled inside the cone, which prevented the fire from damaging the seeds. The seeds themselves remained attached to the cone until it had cooled down enough for them to spill out. It's one thing to read about this, but to see it in action – to see the cone open itself up in the flames really makes you understand how the forest needs fire in order to sustain itself.

The necessity of regular fires in the forest was, until recently, such a little-understood thing that people coming to the forest naturally went to great lengths to *prevent* them. Fire has always provoked great fear in mankind, and it can be hard to believe that its devastating effects could actually have a positive and vital outcome.

There are about 9,000 forest fires recorded annually in Canada, the vast majority of them the result of natural phenomena such as lightning strikes. Over the course of a year over two million hectares of forest will be burned.

By way of comparison, over 800,000 hectares of forest are felled every year. Incidentally, by far the worst threat the forest faces is insect infestation; for example, outbreaks of spruce budworm caused extensive damage between 1980 and 1993, and over 6.6 million hectares in the eastern boreal forest was affected.

It's not just the trees that are able to recover from a fire; the new growth coming from scorched and blackened ground, enriched with nutrients released by the flames, provides good grazing for moose. The moose population thrives in the aftermath of a forest fire, happily eating the young green shoots of fireweed – what we, in Britain, call rosebay willowherb. Insects can benefit too, especially highly specialised ones such as the black fire-beetle, which has to track down newly burnt wood on which to lay its eggs, and can do so nowhere else.

For the many tribes that once inhabited the forest, the threat of fire destroying their homes was a serious one, but they lived in such a way that they were able to move quickly away from danger. This was their home, though, and to think of it as a wilderness – as we do today – is incorrect. They adapted to a way of life that was completely natural to them, and the abundance of the forest met all of their needs. It was home to them, every bit as much as a farm would be to a rural dweller today. Both live off the land and create comforts that make a place a home. Indeed, there is no First Nation word for wilderness – it's just not as alien to them as it has become to us. Interestingly, too, they have no word for 'outdoors', because there is no delineation between being out of doors and in. That's the kind of thing that really interests me – the knowledge, the skills that I acquired, which make me feel completely at home, at one, with a wild place like this.

BIRCH-BARK BITING

I met Sally Milne, a Cree craftswoman from Saskatchewan, who showed me the amazing craft of bark-biting, which she had learned as a child while living in the forest. She separates layers of birch bark, as if peeling away the backing on thin sheets of sticky plastic, and then folds the sheets into small triangles, which she bites. The marks she makes with her teeth create beautiful patterns, as elegant as any stained-glass window. This technique was originally adopted so that people could make templates for needlecraft, and patterns to adorn their baskets and clothing, but it's now become its own form of craft. Sally produced an amazing image of four bees around a flower for me, all in the space of a few moments.

Watching her fingers work carefully with the thin bark, I was pretty sure I'd find this tricky, and I was right. When it was my turn, I had to move the bark slowly as I bit down, trying to widen the hole without going right through, but when I unfolded my effort, I was pretty pleased. It wasn't as neat as Sally's, but held up against the autumnal sunlight it was still a lovely image.

'Some kind of a flower,' Sally said kindly. 'Maybe something native to England that I've never seen,' she added.

'Hmm ... a Tudor rose,' I suggested.

Sally had been taught this skill by her grandmother when she was very small, and she is determined to ensure that it survives in the modern world. 'All the native people across the boreal forest knew about it,' she said, 'some better than others.'

As a child, she would sit with her grandmother and cousins to make 'bitings'; it was a regular and productive pastime for them all, and doing it today reminds her of her childhood. Her grandmother was quite specific about the way the patterns had to be formed, with a flower at the centre and four identical items – like the bees in the biting I had in my hand – around it to balance the whole picture.

Sally's designs are balanced this way because they are symbolic of a belief in the balance of the world – a concept taught by Black Elk, a Sioux Indian who had, as a small boy, been at the Battle of Little Big Horn, and had even travelled to England with Buffalo Bill in the 1880s. Black Elk's words were translated by his son for a New York writer, who wrote them down:

All our power came to us from the sacred
hoop of the nation and so long as the
hoop was unbroken the people flourished.
The flowering tree was the living centre
of the hoop and the circle of the four
quarters nourished it. The East of the
hoop gave peace and light, the South
gave warmth, the West gave rain and the
North with its cold and mighty wind,
gave strength and endurance.

Sally's pictures strongly reflect this ideal.

'The forest is home to me – I love being in the forest,' she told me. 'It's everything.'

Sally grew up in the forest, and she's absolutely fearless. Even bears fail to worry her. 'They don't bother you if you don't bother them', she said lightly, but the little chuckle that followed suggested otherwise.

'A healthy respect for your environment, that's all the safety you need in the forest. Bad weather, thin ice, slippery rocks, fast water, the wind – you know, when you live in an environment, what to be aware of when you're out there.'

Sally can't emphasise enough the importance of respecting the environment. Even when cutting bark from the birch trees for her bitings, she is careful to remove only the topmost layers, to avoid damaging the trees. The forest provides a perfectly balanced ecosystem for all who live there, and always has done. Despite its breadth, seeming inhospitability and potential dangers, it became a safe and plentiful home for those who lived in tandem with its natural cycles.

And then, one day, into that enormous wild space, came the palest of faces: a European.

CHAPTER 2

THE FUR TRADE

The first explorers to navigate their way around the bays and inlets of what would one day become Canada were Italians. But the first to set foot on Canadian soil were Frenchmen in the 1530s. Intrepid explorer Jacques Cartier (1491–1557), who would later claim Canadian soil for France, ventured deep into the waterways around the St Lawrence River, and in 1583, English nobleman and explorer Sir Humphrey Gilbert (1539–1583) claimed Newfoundland for England. It wasn't until the early part of the following century that a permanent settlement was established by French navigator Samuel de Champlain (1567–1635) on the site of what is now Quebec City, which coincided with England's establishment of a colony

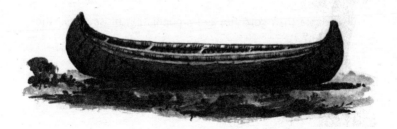

in 1607, far to the south in Virginia.

Initial enthusiasm for the voyages of discovery to the New World waned when it appeared that the get-rich-quick dreams that had inspired them were not going to be realised. The voyages had been instigated because of the universal belief that they would produce a new route to the riches of the Far East; Europeans also hoped to make a similar discovery to that of the Spanish, who had found plentiful gold and silver in South America.

Instead, the travellers encountered harsh climates, impenetrable forests and seemingly ferocious native people, which was, to say the least, off-putting. However, the discoveries made by Samuel de Champlain changed that point of view dramatically. For Samuel de Champlain had discovered something that would prove to be even more valuable than gold: fur, and a population of 'savages' who were prepared to hunt and trade it.

The late 16th and early 17th centuries were unrivalled eras of expansion in Europe. By the time the Victorian era arrived, Britain's empire was well established, and it was the job of the army and the civil service to manage this vast collection of colonies across the globe. But, in the centuries preceding that, it was the acquisition of empire rather than its consolidation that drove the ships of Britain's Navy and the colonists who left her shores. There was obviously a fascinating mindset then – people were prepared to travel into the unknown, they were prepared to risk unbelievable hardships and even their lives, without knowing exactly what it was they were searching for.

Yes, of course they were interested in wealth, in the acquisition of gold or other precious metals; but it wasn't only this that drove them on, any more than it was missionary zeal to 'convert the heathen'. This was a time of transition, falling between the end of medieval superstition and the dawn of the Age of Enlightenment, a time in history when rational philosophies swept the continent of Europe, from the works of Francis Bacon (1561–1626) and Thomas Hobbes (1588–1679) to René Descartes (1596–1650) and Baruch Spinoza (1632–1677). Descartes' famous phrase *cogito ergo sum* ('I think, therefore I am') reduced all certainties to one undeniable fact – that knowledge was everything.

The creation of the empire came about as England – for the nation of Britain hadn't yet been fully realised – sought to establish trade and new sources of the raw materials that were proving necessary to its growing population. Perhaps most importantly of all, England sought to keep up with the other European nations that were surging across the oceans to establish their own empires – Portugal, Spain and France.

HENRY HUDSON AND NEW FRANCE

While the French expanded into Canada along the waterways of the St Lawrence River, the English sought a passage around the top of Canada – the fabled Northwest Passage, which would allow for a safe and speedy route across the Atlantic and the Pacific to the Far East. Sir Francis Drake (1540–1596) had failed to find a route in his circumnavigation of the globe, instead touching land on the northwest coast of North America, possibly as far south as California, but maybe as high up as Vancouver Island. The exact location is unknown because the English decided to

falsify the maps to keep the location of 'Nova Albion' a secret from the Spanish, and now no one is able to determine the exact place he reached.

The search for the Northwest Passage resumed under Henry Hudson (1565–1611), an English sea explorer and navigator who opened up parts of the Arctic Ocean and north-eastern North America. He had initially sailed upriver from the coast, believing, after conversations with the native people, that the sea could be reached; however, his journey failed when he realised that he could go no further. The river on which he travelled – the Hudson River – is named after him, and its mouth lies in one of the greatest American cities: New York. It seems likely that the 'sea' to which the native people referred was the Great Lakes that lay to the north.

Undeterred, Hudson set out to try again. In 1610, he sailed around the southern tip of Greenland and entered the vast bay that opens up at the top of Newfoundland. That winter, which he spent mapping the coastline of the bay, his boat became stuck in the ice. In the spring of 1611, his crew mutinied and he was set loose on a small boat, along with his teenaged son and some eight members of his crew. He was never seen again, and the bay he entered now bears his name: Hudson Bay.

The crew members of his ship, the aptly named *Discovery*, returned to London. Unusually for mutineers, they were not hanged; perhaps it was decided that the maps and charts they returned with, together with the knowledge they had of the land and the conditions of Hudson Bay, provided such valuable information that it outweighed the lives of the men they'd cast adrift. This kind of pragmatic decision was to govern much of English policy towards the growth of its empire over the next century; it most certainly ruled the English reaction to the French occupation of the land to the south. The majority of the eastern parts of Canada continued to be held by France up to the end of the 17th century. The northern and western parts were completely unexplored by Europeans until then, and the central parts only so far as they impinged on the developing nation further south. Small wars and skirmishes between Britain and the French, and their respective allies amongst the First Nations, continued.

The French presence in Canada had commenced when the fishing grounds off the Canadian coast encouraged trading missions to come ashore to meet the local native populations. The French sailors returned home with something that was to change the interior of Canada forever: beaver fur coats. These coats, which they traded for trinkets they'd brought from Europe, kept the fishermen warm in the cold. When they returned to Europe, it didn't take long for hat-makers to realise the potential of the fur in these coats to be turned into the felt that made the best hats.

Beaver fur was to become one of the most valuable trading commodities in the world – particularly when trappers realised the massive extent of the beaver population living in the rivers and lakes of Canada, and the potential for a huge income from the sale of their pelts for hat-making. In the days before umbrellas, a waterproof hat was vital.

Until this time, beaver pelts had come from Russia, but hunting there had been overtaken by commercial exploitation, pushing up the price of beaver pelts and decimating the beaver population. The seemingly endless flow of furs from Canada – once the trade opened up in the coming decades – revitalised the business, and the need for almost anyone who could afford it to have a felt hat made from beaver ensured that a steady stream of travellers departed from Canada's shores into the hinterland, seeking new sources of the profitable fur.

HAT-MAKING

The process of making a hat from beaver pelt was complex and required many stages. One of the early parts of the process was preparing the fur, which involved the use of mercury and the manual removal of the guard hairs. When the hairs were removed and the wool shaved off the pelt, the mercury vapour was released. Long-term exposure to the mercury caused serious health problems for the hatters, as it attacked their nervous systems. They grew unsteady on their feet, they struggled to think and talk, and their muscles began to twitch. This is the origin of the phrase 'mad as a hatter'.

Beaver fur was so highly prized that the floor of the hat-maker's workshop would be covered with sand. At night the sand would be swept up and sifted, so that any hairs that had fallen from the worktables could be collected up and reused.

Next, time was spent carding, bowing, matting, basoning, planking, blocking, dyeing, waterproofing and stiffening the hat, which was then brushed and lined before being sold. It was an exhausting process that explained, in part, why a beaver fur hat was such a treasured possession.

Beaver fur was soft, durable, waterproof, warm and attractive. Most importantly, however, it had become a 'social necessity', and remained so from the mid-1600s until the 1830s, changing in style with the moods of fashion. This fed the market, and the demand became relentless. In fact, some liken the scramble to cash in on the vast Canadian beaver market to a gold rush, such was the feverish desire to bring back the best pelts. Many hundreds of men lost their lives in the process. It was this demand that changed what was once an economic backwater into a massive global industry. And it did so almost overnight.

A TUG-OF-WAR FOR TRADE

Initially, the French colonists set up home on the banks of the Saguenay River in Quebec, which drains into the larger St Lawrence. Here a trading post was established to receive the furs brought in by native people. The furs were then packaged up and sent back to Europe. The French were determined to establish official sites at which the trade would be conducted, which would allow them to monitor the movement of fur, goods and people. As a result of the trade, the entire St Lawrence was opened, all the way to the Great Lakes in the north.

A tug-of-war soon developed between France and Britain, as these two countries fought over this land and

control of the valuable fur trade. The tribes along the rivers and in the woods, the Huron and the Iroquois, soon became involved in the conflict.

Although the French had a head start in developing the trade, which they hoped to control through their trading posts, they had reckoned without the spirit of enterprise that was to characterise the development and opening up of Canada. It soon became clear that where there was a profit to be made, there were plenty of people willing to bypass the rules. No group was more emblematic of this fact than the first of the groups that would provide the fur trade with its legendary figures and most important tool – the *coureurs de bois* and the birch-bark canoe.

RUNNERS OF THE WOODS

The *coureurs de bois* – literally, the runners of the woods – were independent adventurers and traders. They made their way – in small groups or even alone – into the heart of the forest (the *pays d'en haute* or 'high country') to do business with the First Nations and to bring back the valuable beaver pelts. To traverse these environments, some of them home to hostile Iroquois, the intrepid Frenchmen used the rivers – fast, furious and difficult to negotiate – and they travelled in canoes made of local birch bark.

When I made my journey to the heart of the fur trade – the waterways around the Great Lakes – I was determined to do so just as the *coureurs de bois* had done, using the skills and tools of woodsmen. The birch canoe makes almost no sound as it slips through the water, and its fastidious construction makes it a joy to manoeuvre. I even managed to run some rapids in my canoe. The strong scent of cedar that rose up as I went into the maelstrom of the rapids was a fabulous reminder of the boat's heritage (see page 50), and brought me closer to the journeys I had set out to recreate – the voyages of the *coureurs de bois*.

I was travelling on the French River, which runs westwards from Lake Nipissing into the eastern bay at the edge of Lake Huron, one of the largest of the Great Lakes. The bay into which the French River flows is, in its own right, large enough to be considered one of the 20 largest lakes in the world.

Lake Huron is a complicated lake to navigate, as over 30,000 islands rise from its waters. It is the fifth-largest freshwater lake in the world, and was named by French travellers in honour of the tribe that troubled them the most on their journeys.

■ ─ ■ ─ ■ ─ ■ ─ ■ ─ ■ ─ ■ ─ ■ ─ ■ ─ ■ ─ ■ ─ ■

The French River is named after those early *coureurs de bois* who paddled down it. It was here that the fur trade began its ascent; on these waterways, the travellers traded with the native people, and collected the valuable pelts before returning to the trading posts on the St Lawrence. The pelts would then be dispatched from the trading posts to Europe, where a voracious market was emerging. The *coureurs de bois* would venture far into the deep woods, paddling along smaller and smaller rivers and creeks, until they were face to face with the people from the First

Nations. This was a useful strategy, as meeting the First Nations people on their own terms and territory made them less hostile, and more open to negotiation. The native people came to expect the frequent visitors, and began to raise their prices as the numbers increased.

The Europeans brought an amazing array of trade goods, introducing the native people to technology such as muskets with shot and powder, traps to help with the hunting of beaver, and copper kettles that revolutionised the lives of Indian women (who were used to boiling water by placing hot rocks into water-filled birch-bark containers). As trade expanded, it was clear that the First Nations people preferred to trade for practical items from Europe. At the outset of the fur trade, ornamental axes that doubled up as pipes were proffered, but these were soon discarded in favour of weapons, awls, hooks for fishing, cooking implements, various cloths and even well-sharpened tomahawks (much like the one I carried with me on my trip).

These European items transformed the lives of the First Nations people, so much so that maybe this is one of the reasons why they were open to the advances of the missionaries who later reached their shores. Having seen evidence of the wondrous gifts that the missionaries' God had offered to the Europeans, they were primed to believe in his existence, and hoped they would be rewarded with similar bounty.

Although the French River is stunningly beautiful – particularly in the sharp morning air that greeted me when I stepped out of my tent – it remains a strange and at times dangerous territory. The *coureurs de bois* relied heavily on the knowledge of those who already lived here, for this hostile land was a potential minefield for newcomers, particularly Europeans who were unfamiliar with the land and its inhabitants.

As well as helping them adjust to life in the forest and on the move, the First Nations had the answer to the biggest problem the *coureurs de bois* faced: how to move the furs from the hunting grounds down to the port of Montreal (originally Mont Real – Mount Royal – when first situated there by the French). The birch-bark canoe was the single most important thing the Europeans would adopt from the First Nations, and it was to enhance and accelerate the growth of the fur trade immeasurably.

THE BIRCH-BARK CANOE

If the United States was opened up by the chuck wagon and the horse, it was undoubtedly the lightweight birch-bark canoe that was responsible for making the exploration of Canada's wild interior possible. Strong enough to run rapids, and light enough to carry when it wasn't possible to paddle any further – a practice that became known as 'portage' – the birch-bark canoe is the ideal tool for a country where rivers are the only highways. In a birch-bark canoe, the rapids are no longer impassable obstacles, but minor inconveniences, easily negotiated by skilled boatsmen at the helm of these wonderful craft.

Birch-bark canoes are sturdy and easily wielded, and they are also easily repaired. When I took my canoe out of the

French River, I accidentally banged it against some rocks. Using resin from nearby trees, mixed with fat to make it malleable – bear fat would traditionally have been used – I managed to patch the canoe and make it watertight again within minutes.

The boats were made with traditional tools – an axe, crooked knife and awl. Cedar, which is light, easy to split and resistant to decay, is a key component of the canoe, and used to form the gunwales and inwales, which are lashed together with rawhide. Sheets of birch bark are unrolled and laid on level, specially cleaned ground, with the white outer layer of bark uppermost. This eventually becomes the inside of the canoe. To enable the bark to be folded evenly upwards all around the frame, slits called gores must be made to allow the bark to overlap in places and prevent bulging. As the bark is bent upwards and starts to take on the required shape, it is secured with upright posts. There is a complicated series of steps to complete the craft, with extra sections of bark added, creating spruce root lacing, pegging and then lacing together the bark additions, providing support for the inwales, and pegging and lacing together the outwale and inwale. Cedar ribs about a centimetre thick are cut and then soaked, making it easier to split.

Thwarts are carved and laced in, and the ribs are heated with boiling water to soften them and make them pliable. Without ribs to support it, the bark hull sags like soft leather. In place, they stretch the bark taut and help to give the canoe its final shape. Thin cedar sheets are placed between the ribs and the bark, giving rigidity to the hull and stretching the bark taut. The ends of the canoe obtain their strength from the stem pieces, which are made by splitting a batten of cedar many times and heating it so that it bends like a laminate into the desired shape. This batten is then split lengthways into two identical pieces. After all the joins in the bark have been sealed with melted spruce resin and bear fat, the canoe can be paddled. And what a joy it is: as light as a feather, and unbelievably easy to manoeuvre in even the most treacherous rapids.

It's easy to see why these canoes became indispensable to the European traders, and why they were, ultimately, the only means by which to achieve fast, efficient travel on the inland waterways. It's interesting to note that none of the technological advances of the Europeans, many of which were happily acquired and used by the First Nations, could match the birch-bark canoe for speed, agility and performance. Perhaps nowhere else in the world was the indigenous technology completely superior to that brought in by foreigners. The traders took this technology and, as we shall see, adapted it to become the lynchpin of the fur trade.

THE DOKIS

The land around the French River was home to the Dokis nation, and I met up with one of them on my travels. Norman Dokis is an extraordinary man. It seemed that the centuries between the Europeans arriving in the woods and the present day simply did not exist for Norman. He spoke to me as if white faces had appeared only very recently. His stories of his tribal people were fresh and lively – almost as if they were his own memories, rather than passed down through generations.

'Our relationship to the forest is deep-rooted,' Norman said. 'We depended upon the forest for everything, and we've had these thousands and thousands of years of knowledge passed on from generation to generation. We know where to gather, to be successful. Life here was very, very hard, and if you didn't know how to survive off the land you wouldn't live very long.

'We embraced the fur trade. It certainly benefited our people in terms of the modern equipment we were able to have; it was easier to start a fire, for instance. And the axe, the knife, the pots and pans – these were revolutionary. The Europeans who came to this country were shown medicinal plants and exactly how to live off this land; that era of first contact was the first dagger into this larger animal we have out here, in terms of the destructive powers that came with the modernisation of European culture.'

But there were also high points, as the two cultures united in trade, and, ultimately, in relationships.

THE MÉTIS

One aspect of European culture that was adopted in the woods was the institution of marriage. The *coureurs de bois* married into the families of the tribes with which they had contact, and the children that came from those relationships have gone on to form one of the largest First Nation tribes there is. Known as 'the Métis', they are now a tribe, a people, and a nation in their own right. In fact, as a nation, they are entitled to the same rights as any one of the First Nations and treated as a unique people in their own right.

The original travellers into the woods had been independent men, driven out of the trading posts by the rules and regulations that they had probably sought to escape by leaving Europe in the first place. It's no surprise that some of them went on to marry native women as a result. However, the French authorities were well aware of the achievements of the *coureurs de bois*, and realised that they were in danger of letting control of the outlying districts of the St Lawrence basin slip out of their grasp. There was nothing they could do to stop the traders they had, after all, helped to establish; and with British immigration into Canada through Newfoundland starting to increase, there was only one answer they could think of to ensure that they remained in control of the fur trade and the land that they plundered. The decision was taken to legitimise the *coureurs de bois* – to control what they did, tax it, and, in doing so, keep a firm hand on the land known then as 'New France'.

Ultimately this was to prove the undoing of the French; the government back in France became obsessed with the concept of turning the land into a useful part of a greater France. The English, however, saw a value in trade, and in creating a vast trade network – allowing commerce to conquer the land for them.

The *coureurs de bois* were disapproved of by Montreal authorities and the royal officials, who preferred the Huron and other First Nations to be involved in the trapping and transportation of the furs, and the settlers to be able to govern the trade. This ensured that the flow of furs into the market was steady, and that the price was kept stable.

The arrival of the *coureurs de bois* destabilised the goods trade in Montreal, for these men would arrive with countless furs to exchange for muskets, clothing, copper pots and alcohol, which they would also trade. Accordingly, in 1681, the authorities granted pardons to the *coureurs de bois* who were trading in its territory without a licence. However, to be granted a pardon the men needed to agree to work under licence for one of the Montreal traders. In this way, the *voyageurs* were created from the *coureurs de bois* and the Métis, and legitimised by the French authorities. These *voyageurs* would go on to change life in the woods dramatically, and thereby alter the heart of Canada itself.

THE VOYAGEURS

For our programme, a group of historians, archivists and enthusiasts from the Canadian Canoe Museum recreated the lives of the *voyageurs*, in particular utilising their mode of transport and dressing as the *voyageurs* did. I spent some time with them, and their leader, Jeremy Ward, made it clear what a tough life they experienced, but how rewarding it was as well.

Being a *voyageur* must have been difficult work – paddling all day while transporting the heavy bundles of beaver pelts. The men were responsible for transporting pelts weighing tons, as well as their own tools, equipment, food and canoes. But being amongst a group of men who relied upon their bushcraft, who relished the activities associated with life in the deep forest, who lived seasonally, just as the forest natives did, must have been exhilarating at times.

On my travels across the Canadian wilderness, I chose to live as the *voyageurs* once did, setting up my camp on the same sites, and adopting the techniques that made survival possible. Like them, I used a tripod set over my fire to cook. This was easy to create, by chopping three sticks – two with forked ends – to an equal length and then leaning them together so that they rested in the forked end. At the other end of my fire I created a bipod – again, branches of an equal width and thickness, one of them forked to hold the other while I tied it down. It didn't need to be as robust as a tripod, because it was merely there to lend support and allow me to use more than one cooking pot across my fire. I placed a crossbar between the two, held in place by the tripod and supported by the bipod, then I used forked sticks to create sturdy hooks on which to hang my kettle and my pot, lashing

it all together with 'withies', which are saplings that I twisted to make them more pliable. I was then ready to start cooking, and I had enough space to use as many pots as I wished, and could make the fire as big as I needed to.

Some *voyageurs* would have left the supports standing when they departed from the camp, because anything that saved time after a hard day's paddling would be welcomed by subsequent travellers. In the native tradition, however, they were dismantled, as it was believed that leaving them *in situ* would bring bad luck. Certainly it would have advised potential enemies of their presence, and so most *voyageurs* removed all traces of their stay.

There was considerable warfare between the First Nations people, a situation not helped by the growth of the fur trade with its rival factions. I was interested to hear that they were one of the harbingers of chemical warfare, albeit rather rudimentary. If they knew the location of their enemy, and the wind was blowing in the appropriate direction, they set fire to poison ivy, whose noxious oils would burn and blister the lungs of the men who breathed it in.

The *voyageurs* set off at daybreak in order to make the most of the long days on the water. To avoid having to build another fire in the morning, I recommend boiling up some water before retiring, and storing it in a thermos for a morning brew. Fresh water boiled over the dying fire will be cool enough to fill a flask the following day. It's likely that the *voyageurs* kept their fires burning into the night, or filled the base with stones that could be used to heat the water come morning. The men carried their food with them, packed tightly in their bags, and prepared as they needed it. Their traditional dish was *rubaboo*, a basic stew or porridge, traditionally made of peas and/or corn with bear or pork fat, and thickened with bread or flour. Pemmican (a concentrated mixture of fats and proteins; see page 89) and maple syrup were also commonly added to the mixture. It was bush food, and whatever was fresh, convenient or local would be thrown into the mixture, which was usually served hot.

NEGOTIATING THE RAPIDS

Heading out for a day's paddling was fine on smooth water, but the prospect of rapids would have been disheartening for the *voyageurs*. I watched as Jeremy Ward and his companions approached the rapids in a traditional *voyageur* way, by beaching the canoe ahead of the wild water, emptying it of its contents, and carrying the canoe and its load past the danger points. The cargo was too valuable to risk negotiating the rapids by canoe, despite the skill of the *voyageurs*, and the heavy load made it harder to manoeuvre. They were travelling in a large canoe, known as a 'Montreal canoe', which they had made by hand at the Canadian Canoe Museum. It was a true work of art, but its size and weight made transporting it on foot difficult and time-consuming.

Beaching and carrying the canoe, known as 'portage', would involve finding open ground over which everything could be transported on foot. One of the men would walk ahead and clear a path, removing any rocks or tree branches. If the portage path were in regular use, it would be marked and open for anyone to use. Portages were often long and arduous, particularly when the *voyageurs* moved on to completely new bodies of water. When they reached the side of the lake or river with their belongings and cargo – downstream from the rapids, or at a new destination – they'd hoist the canoe out of the water, invert it over their shoulders, and carry it to their new launch site.

The necessity for regular portage was just one reason why the birch-bark canoes were so valuable in this land: their construction, the materials from which they were made, and their versatility, made the task as easy as possible. I have done it myself, and I've sometimes felt that I'm in another country entirely after two decent portages. Small, remote creeks and unknown lakes were suddenly accessible, and there were literally no obstacles preventing the transportation of the beaver pelt.. Only canoes can be portaged and that's what made them the only craft capable of opening up this land.

THE MONTREAL CANOE

Montreal canoes, or *canots du maître*, are specially adapted, elongated birch-bark canoes that were used by the *voyageurs*. They were large enough to carry the quantity of trade goods required to sell to the trappers, and equally large enough to transport the furs back to Montreal. Their size also made them safer on the open waters of the lakes, which were more readily visited as new routes opened up. About 10 to 12 metres long, the Montreal canoe was manned by between six and 14 *voyageurs*, with the front man leading the stroke, and the man at the rear employing his paddle as a rudder. The canoes travelled in groups of three or four, with a guide leading the way.

These were massive boats, weighing some 90 kilograms empty, which is light enough to allow them to be carried over the portages. Fully loaded, however, the canoes weighed about four tons each, and would complete about 2,000 kilometres on each trip. At this weight they didn't lend themselves to portage as easily as the smaller versions, and a series of portages could tack weeks on to tight schedules.

It's not surprising that the *voyageurs* were eager to find alternatives to portage. In some cases, the boat would remain on the water, with the cargo discharged and carried on foot. It would then be guided through the rapids by men walking ahead of the boat, leading it on a rope. Some of the *voyageurs* stayed on board and poled the canoe safely through the churning, icy water. This technique was known as 'lining'.

I encouraged Jeremy and his crew to try lining through a particularly rough part on the river, and we were all thrilled to find it successful. But it was hard work. The rocks they used to lever the boat forward had been worn smooth by the running water, and it was difficult to get purchase on them, let alone negotiate a safe passage. It's amazing to

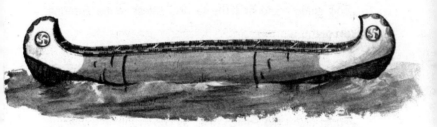

think that they were probably the first people in over a century to travel that route up the river, in a canoe of that size. Seeing Jeremy and his team re-enacting the techniques of *voyageurs* as we made the TV series was, at some points, like watching ghosts.

The sheer weight of Montreal canoes made travelling

across the open waters of lakes hazardous, although the rapids in the shallow, fast-flowing rivers were treacherous too. Winds often blew up, whipping large waves over the edge of the boats and sinking them. The canoes would tend to hug the shorelines, but this could extend a journey by days, costing the *voyageurs* money and requiring more provisions. It was a delicate balancing act, which is one reason why the guides were so well paid and valuable. A good guide could find the fastest, safest route, ensuring optimum profits for all.

Trade blossomed with the advent of the big Montreal canoes, but the downside of this was that the beaver became extinct along the French River as opportunistic *voyageurs* scooped up any animals they spotted on their routes into and out of the trading posts. New areas would have to be explored to find more of the precious beaver pelts.

SASH-WEAVING

I noticed that many of Jeremy's men were wearing brightly coloured sashes around their waists, and I knew from the paintings of the *voyageurs* I'd studied that these were authentic. Like so many items used by those in the fur trade, the sashes were created using skills inherited from the First Nations, and they truly are a beauty to behold. They were worn as belts, folded over to make a pocket. Some people believe they held in the hernias thought to be a side-effect of the strenuous work the *voyageurs* undertook.

I wanted to see for myself how they were made, and to learn why they were so important for the *voyageurs*, so I went to see Carol James, who still weaves them today. They are known as 'finger-woven sashes', and she told me that they would originally have been made using buffalo hair and grasses. The arrival of the Europeans brought spun, multi-coloured threads, which were subsequently used. Traditional sashes were made from a worsted thread, meaning that all of the threads were aligned together, making the final product enormously hard-wearing.

Carol struggles to obtain the proper worsted thread she needs nowadays. She imports it from Sweden, re-twists it to make it stronger, and then dyes it herself. One sash can take almost nine months to make, but the end result is worth the effort. Not only are these sashes beautiful in their own right, but the efforts of Carol and other weavers has helped to ensure that the traditional craft remains alive.

She showed me the process of weaving the sash-cloth, using a beautifully coloured piece of cloth. It was suspended at eye level, with a mass of threads hanging below, waiting to be twisted into place. There were 286 threads in each sash, said Carol, and she demonstrated how they were woven together by nimbly moving her fingers through the threads, pulling one from the back to lay it over its neighbour, and working her way from the centre of the cloth to the edge.

The whole process could be stopped and started as needed, which reflects the fact that the weavers – the *voyageurs* and their wives – often had a nomadic existence, and would have only a moment here or there to complete the work.

'Human beings,' said Carol, 'are meaning-seeking creatures, not just a collection of tissues and bones. We're a whole and we need to maintain our heritage to feel connected and as one.' This is one reason why Carol weaves her sashes in a hospital in Winnipeg, where the patients can be inspired by seeing a part of their heritage on show, and feel a sense of peace as they are drawn into the process of the weaving.

Carol is not just a marvellous lady, but someone who I would describe as a rock in the river. Every time you see a rock, you stop and take note. You move on, but the rock will always be there – and it should be remembered.

CANOES AND CANADA

It's great to be able to see the skills of the fur trade in use today, particularly in the place where they were first developed, and where they formed a part of daily life. With that in mind, I went to meet someone who feels much the same way that I do.

Author and canoe expert Kevin Callan knows that the French River is a quieter place today than it was back in the days of the *voyageurs*. In earlier times, it was a highway – a route for the large Montreal canoes to come roaring down just as truckers do today. But none of that would have been possible without the skills acquired from the First Nations people, and the versatile canoes that they produced.

'The canoe is made for travelling the wilderness,' said Kevin, 'because you can portage it.' He is insistent that the canoe is the single most important symbol of Canada, because the country simply would not exist without the exploration that was possible once it was adopted as the prime mode of transport. In fact, he suggests that the canoe rather than the maple leaf should feature on the Canadian flag.

'The canoe made Canada and it is still making Canada,' he said. To Kevin, the sight of a canoe on top of a car,

Approaching Grey Owl's remote cabin on snowshoes.

Beavers raise their body temperature to allow them to swim for longer in the icy water.

Temporary shelter made by stacking dead branches against a fallen tree trunk.

A beaver lodge in winter, where it's only just visible as a bump poking through the ice, and in summer.

A beaver lodge in summer.

The bark of Trembling Aspen trees is not only beautiful but also enormously important to survival in the wilderness, not least as a source of raw material for making canoes.

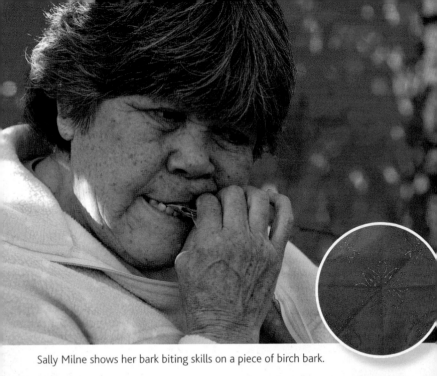

Sally Milne shows her bark biting skills on a piece of birch bark.

Wild rice is a high-protein grain that's rich in vitamins and minerals.

Riding the rapids in a birch-bark canoe.

The type of goods that would have been traded for furs.

A cooking tripod made from paddles, as shown in a Paul Kane illustration.

heading off for the weekend, is not just a sign of recreation but a way of life in Canada.

I agree that the canoe is a terrific symbol of the making of Canada but it's not the only thing that could challenge the maple leaf on the country's flag. The men who paddled those canoes were also responsible for creating this great land, and, for me, there are two *voyageurs* in particular who stand out: Pierre Radisson and Médard des Groseilliers. It was their initiative and entrepreneurial spirit that led to the creation of the company that would one day serve as the backbone of Canadian trade and exploration.

These *voyageurs* set out to shorten the long route through the lakes and up the St Lawrence River to Montreal with the heavy loads of pelts. Wouldn't it be better, they theorised, if the *voyageurs* could simply take the pelts they'd traded up to the edge of Hudson Bay? Not only would this be quicker for the woodsmen, but ships travelling back to Europe would have a much faster journey from the bay, provided that they weren't trapped by ice.

Their idea was rejected by the authorities in Montreal.

They didn't want to expand the fur trade any more by opening up new avenues for the *voyageurs* to follow; instead, they planned to concentrate on farming and the benefits that would bring. So, Radisson and des Groseilliers took their plan to the other main power in Canada – the English.

THE ENGLISH ARRIVE

There are many remarkable moments in this story, and this is one of them. When Radisson and des Groseilliers brought their plan to England in 1668, London had recently lost hundreds of thousands of its population, through the plague and the Great Fire. The city was very much in mourning; however, it was also a time of regeneration and regrowth, and the *voyageurs*' extraordinary idea was met with great enthusiasm. Their first port of call was Prince Rupert, a cousin of King Charles II. He loved the project, and set about involving Charles and a number of other wealthy men in

its sponsorship. These two Frenchmen and their mad idea could easily have been turned down, and the money saved for safer enterprises close to home. However, the idea was embraced, and one of the greatest companies in the world was formed. This company would become one of the most important reasons why Canada remained independent from the United States, and became a strong, wealthy country in its own right.

Radisson and des Groseilliers set sail back to Canada in the ships *Nonsuch* and *The Eaglet*; *The Eaglet* had to abandon the journey, but the *Nonsuch*, with des Groseilliers aboard, made it across the Atlantic. The ship returned to England the following year, having made a successful trading voyage to the furthest south-easterly point in the bay. The two Frenchmen were proved right. The journey was speedy, and profits could be massive. Accordingly, the Hudson's Bay Company was formed, and Canada's future was assured.

CHAPTER 3

THE HUDSON'S BAY COMPANY

The Hudson's Bay Company – which was founded on 2nd May 1670, when King Charles II granted a charter to his cousin Prince Rupert and his associates – is not just Canada's foremost and most influential trader. The success of the HBC is also largely responsible for the existence of Canada as an independent nation. Today, Canada's unique culture and diverse population exist because this royal charter and the subsequent activities of the HBC saved the country from becoming just another state in the union of the United States.

The charter of 1670 made the Hudson's Bay Company 'true and absolute Lordes and Proprietors' of Rupert's Land – the name given to all of the land draining into Hudson

Bay, a huge area of northern and western Canada. It was named for Prince Rupert, who became the company's first governor. The land outlined in the charter is equal to almost 2.6 million square kilometres of Canada, which comprises more than 40 per cent of the modern nation. Charles believed that the land was his to give because no other Christian monarch had claimed it.

The charter that granted rights to the Hudson's Bay Company allowed them rights to exploit not just the fur trade, but also all of the land and the waterways that drained into the bay. Effectively, this established the company's dominion over a huge percentage of the viable land that would one day be Canada. The granting of this charter also shows how little was known about the country back then, because it must go down in history as one of the most magnificent gifts ever made. In one fell swoop, the company acquired vast tracts of land and an extraordinary number of rights on it. Even more amazingly, in return for this gift, the HBC gave only a simple pledge that any member of the Royal Family would receive two elk and two beaver whenever he or she visited the company's territory.

Nearly three centuries later, the company, with its Latin motto of *pro pelle cutem* ('a skin for a skin'), is still going strong, and the charter is on show in the company's headquarters in Toronto. I went there to meet the company's historian, Joan Murray, and she told me that the hyperbole involved in discussing the history of the HBC is justified. 'The company has a unique role, not just in Canada, but I'd venture to say also in the world,' she said. 'No other company's history is so intertwined with the development

of the history and political life of a country as the HBC is in Canada.'

She's not alone in thinking this. John Buchan, probably best known now as the writer of *The 39 Steps*, was also Governor General of Canada in the late 1930s, and he wrote, 'The Hudson's Bay is not an ordinary commercial company, but a kind of kingdom by itself, and it needs statesmen to administer it.'

'Because Canada was opened up from east to west, first by the French and then by the English,' continued Joan, 'and because HBC held sway, it was inevitable that the company would become very involved with exploration. As a result, the company's influence is inseparable from the development of Canada as a whole.'

EARLY POSTS

The *Nonsuch*, with the brains behind the HBC, des Groseilliers, aboard, was forced by the weather to over-winter by the side of Hudson Bay. He and his men set up a post on land nearby, and once spring had opened up the waterways, nearly 300 First Nations people came up in their canoes, bearing fur to trade. Although the profit on this first trip was negligible, the fact that it had been accomplished was enough, and Charles II signed the famous deed, granting land to the HBC. It read as follows:

> *We do grant unto the said Governor and Company and their successors the sole trade and commerce of all those Seas Straights Bays Rivers Lakes Creeks and Sounds that lie within the entrance of Hudson's Straights and make create and constitute 'them' the true and absolute Lords and Proprietors of the same Territory.*

Four weeks after the charter received royal assent, in May 1670, two ships – the *Wivenhoe* and *Prince Rupert* – set sail to establish a permanent trading post.

The key to making the most profit from the fur trade was to get the furs to Europe as quickly as possible. With its new, shorter route into the heart of the fur country, through the vast inland sea that opened straight into the Atlantic, the HBC had that advantage. But there was another one, too. The traders also found it easier to bring goods deeper into the inland waterways than to Montreal, and the trade goods were also more quickly and easily replenished as well. All in all, the HBC not only controlled the vast majority of the fur trade's land, but held most of the cards when it came to pleasing the traders themselves.

YORK FACTORY

The first of the trading posts the Company set up was in the lower south-east corner of the bay; originally called Charles Fort, it was situated on the mouth of the Rupert River. The building that came to epitomise the HBC, however, was York

Factory, which was established in 1684. The term 'factory' simply meant 'fortified enclosure', and no manufacturing was undertaken at the site, as the name suggests. The factories were home to the 'factors', the officers in charge of trading with the hunters.

Ships from London anchored about 11 kilometres off York Factory, at a place called Five Fathom Hole. Sloops carried in trade goods, and returned laden with furs from here. It would have been a bleak, lonely posting when the first of the HBC's employees were sent to the newly built factories. The biting cold was one of their worst enemies. Hudson's Bay was colder than the oceans to the north, and even colder than the North Pole, as it did not receive the ocean currents that stirred the warmer waters, or brought warmer air in their wake. What's more, the HBC made the rather incredible decision not to heat the posts, to avoid too many people hanging around them doing nothing. Their aim was to ensure that those coming in with things to sell would quickly move on, and back to the central task of trapping beaver. Subsequently, the factors wrote to the committee in London, to draw attention to the cold they endured. They wrote things like:

> *Insufferable cold. Almost froze my arm*
> *in bed. Very troublesome to write, ink*
> *freezing in my pen.*
> *Frozen feet and no wonder, as the*
> *thermometer for the last three nights was*
> *−36, −42, and −38.*

The cold was almost impossible to bear, despite the clothing with which the factors were supplied to wear in the trading posts. This included: an outer garment of moose-skin, with cuffs and a cape of beaver, marten or fox; breeches cut from deerskin, lined with flannel over three layers of cut-up blankets; and shoes of tough leather wrapped round the instep and fastened securely. If they ventured outside, they would add more layers, although there was no guarantee that they would get very far.

'Men cannot see a hundred yards to windward – neither

can one get out of the gates for snow,' one factor wrote to head office. Even when it wasn't snowing the weather was hardly charitable, with storms bringing in 'hail the size of a musket ball'.

Even today, it's quite a challenge to visit York Factory, and the park's website advises visitors to take a great deal of care:

> *Weather conditions are unpredictable at York Factory and can force a longer than anticipated stay. Be sure to take warm clothing, rubber boots, bug repellent, and two or three days of extra supplies. Average temperature for June-July-August: 13°C; a severe temperature drop is common in June and July when the wind comes off the frozen Hudson Bay. There is a 40 per cent chance of daily rain. High winds are frequently experienced; tides up to 4 metres are experienced.*

More ominously, the visitor is warned to be aware of the threat of polar bears.

Nevertheless, within 12 years of the first trips into the Bay, the HBC was generating a profit of 200 per cent on

invested capital. And what of the two Frenchmen at the heart of the enterprise? They both had their gripes with the company. Des Groseilliers eventually sided with the French and died before the end of the century, having sought to seize HBC territory back for New France. Radisson was more fickle, and switched sides a few times – first capturing HBC pelts to sell to the French, and then changing sides again and forcing his nephew to hand over 20,000 pelts to him and the HBC. He eventually settled in England, where he became naturalised, and he died in London in 1710. Neither trader was a direct beneficiary of their extraordinary idea, and the disappointment of playing such a small role in the company's success left them dispirited and even traitorous.

ORCADIANS

The Hudson's Bay Company was owned and operated by rich businessmen and -women in London (Lady Margaret Drax, an attractive and adventurous member of English society, was one of the initial investors), but was very largely staffed by men from the Orkney Isles. The Orkneys lie about 16 kilometres off the northeast coast of Scotland, above the 59th parallel. In many respects, the Islands were the geographical and climactic equal to the inland sea of Hudson Bay, and it was believed that Orkney men would be hardy enough to withstand the elements and get on with the job at hand.

The men who travelled across the sea to work for the HBC were on five-year contracts, so they couldn't depart when the worst weather set in. Chances are, however, that they had the resources to deal with the cold, bleak weather, having had a similar experience at home.

'Orkneymen seemed to fit the bill quite well,' said Joan Murray.

These men became known as 'Orcadians', and they were to prove invaluable to the company. For one thing, they were happy to share their own knowledge of survival in almost intolerable cold and damp. For another, they were able to provide a practical solution to a major problem that arose when the fur trade developed and grew with the expansion of the trading posts. On the open areas of Hudson Bay, the canoes proved vulnerable to the wind and the waves, so a new, larger, more stable boat was required. The HBC used the designs of a boat familiar to the Orcadians, and turned it into something practical for the purposes of the traders: the York boat.

The York boat traversed the bay for over a century and was the main means of transporting furs between inland trading posts and York Factory, after which it was named. It was based upon an Orkney design that was itself based on the old Viking longboats, and its chief benefit was its capacity. Each York boat could carry about three times the amount of cargo that the larger canoes could, and because it was flat-bottomed, it could travel deep into the inlets and creeks as well. At over 12 metres in length, it had a square sail that enabled it to move swiftly over the open waters of the bay. Obviously it was too heavy to carry in portage, but if the crew had no alternative, it could be rolled across the ground over logs to move it from one point to another.

The extent to which the Company relied on the Orcadians is clearer towards the end of the 18th century.

By 1800, 390 of the Company's 498 officers and servants came from the Orkney Islands. Most of the remaining staff (including almost all of the officers) were English. Although a few employees from Orkney had been employed as early as 1701, the first official efforts to employ Orcadians came in 1727, from the Governor at Albany, Joseph Myatt. He wrote to the HBC's committee in London, recommending 'sober' Orcadians over those from London who appeared 'acquainted with the ways and debaucheries of the town.'

Why did the Orcadians go? According to one Orkney-based priest, writing in the 1790s, they went 'from a restlessness of disposition, a desire of change'. They were also offered better wages than those offered by the farmers. At the time that the priest was writing, the HBC paid £6 a year to each ordinary man, as well as offering board, lodging, and a basic set of clothing. In the Orkneys, ordinary farm workers would probably earn around half that, without the clothing allowance. Once the immigrants had learned new skills — say, as a canoeman — then their pay would rise accordingly, and in some cases substantially so. If they travelled as a boat-builder, they might earn £20 or even £30 a year. Some Orcadians would eventually return home wealthy enough to buy their own crofts.

WARS BETWEEN THE ENGLISH AND THE FRENCH

The wars that seemed to rage almost continuously between Britain and France throughout the 18th century spilled over into the rivers and bays of Canada, and trading posts changed hands often as each side's star rose or fell. With the establishment of the first trading posts around Hudson Bay, the fur trade had been effectively split: the English, in the form of the HBC, were in Hudson Bay, while the French remained in Montreal. With the competition this presented, it was necessary for the HBC's rivals to develop further the usefulness of the canoe, enabling them to carry larger loads back from the inland waterways out to the trading posts. This is why the Montreal canoe (see pages 59–60), the 'supertanker' of the fur trade, was developed.

The guides who governed the expeditions of the Montreal canoes took responsibility for any losses, and these were mostly the result of the two main problems that continually dogged the fur trade. The first was the ongoing wars in Europe between Britain and France, which also spilled over to affect the North American colonies and trading areas. Secondly, there was a constant rivalry between the original pioneers of the fur trade, and the powerful newcomers in the shape of the HBC; at times, this erupted into violence.

Between 1694 and 1697, the French and English battled

for control of the original York Factory. Under the command of Pierre Le Moyne d'Iberville, the French captured York Factory in 1694, lost it to the English in 1696, recaptured it the following year, and renamed it Fort Bourbon. It remained under French control until the signing of the Treaty of Utrecht in 1713, which awarded the Hudson's Bay Company exclusive trading rights on Hudson Bay. York Factory quickly became the Company's single most important trading post on the Bay, although its monopoly was successfully challenged by traders from New France who had established a series of posts far to the south in the Lake Superior and Lake Winnipeg regions.

In 1714, HBC employee James Knight returned to York Factory to claim it back from the French, finding 'a quaint cluster of rickety shacks manned by a wretched crew of just nine French defenders, including a chaplain, a surgeon and an apprentice.' As well as being horrified by the cold, he was appalled by the insect life. He wrote: 'Here is now such swarms of such a small sand flyes that we can hardly see the sun through them ... they fly into our ears nose eyes mouth and down our throats as we be most sorely plagued with them.'

Over the next three decades, the HBC seemed to invite the problems that it would later face in the second half of the 18th century. One disillusioned officer later labelled this period as the company's 'long sleep by the Frozen Sea'. They tried to increase trade in a passive way, with the factors content to stay inside their trading posts and wait for the trappers and hunters to bring the furs to them.

Life in the posts wasn't all hardship. James Knight described the geese, pork, sides of beef, hares, fruit preserves and hogsheads of beer he provided to his men for a three-day Christmas feast. They may have been cold and bitten by insects, but the employees were most certainly not starving. Drinking, however, was becoming an increasing problem. The HBC tried to ban it altogether, but brandy was brought ashore anyhow, and it was almost impossible to prevent it being smuggled in for the men. This was not, however, brandy as we know it; instead, it was cheap, coloured gin meant for trade, and its poor quality was the cause of digestive and neurological problems in some of the men who drank it.

When the furs were brought in, the HBC paid a set figure for their worth, which was normally revised on an annual basis. For example, one made beaver (a 'made beaver' was one full pelt) was equivalent to one copper kettle, 20 steel fishing hooks or about a kilogram of Brazilian tobacco (which was deemed far superior to North American-grown strains); 12 made beaver could be traded for one musket.

After almost 31 years of relative peace, the conflict between England and France flared up again between 1753 and 1763 with the Seven Years' War. Tensions had also been rising in 'Rupert's Land', thanks to the shifting balance of the population. Catholic France was keen to develop the region while keeping an eye on its religious health, so that those who wished to flee religious persecution in France were not able to emigrate there. Meanwhile, in Protestant England, religious dissenters were encouraged to move across the Atlantic, as the English government seemed happier to allow the development of a society based more on the principles of trade than those of old, aristocratic Europe.

As a result, the English-speaking population was increasing, while the French-speaking populace remained mostly static. When war eventually broke out, with both sides using the First Nations populations against each other in the tussle for supremacy, a number of heroes appeared. Most notable of these were General James Wolfe, an English general whose death in the battle to take the city of Quebec established his name, and a young American, George Washington, who assisted the English in driving out the French further south.

This time the English were triumphant and a settlement was agreed. France would allow the English rule of Rupert's Land, from the St Lawrence to the far reaches of the west, while the English were prepared to concede some of the sugar-cane islands of the Caribbean, such as Martinique, to the French. While some critics have claimed that this deal was unfair, it's hard to see how and to whom. One byproduct of the agreement was, however, the need for the English to raise funds to pay for the war, something they decided

to do through taxation. The result? The War of American Independence, and the loss of huge swathes of English land.

A large part of Britain's success in the Seven Years' War came from the determination of William Pitt the Elder, and his vision of how the war should be pursued. William Pitt (called 'the Elder', to distinguish him from his son of the same name) was a British Whig statesman who achieved his greatest fame as Prime Minister of Britain during the Seven Years' War, and again several years later. He ensured that the British side of the war was fought with large numbers of troops and professional generals. When the war was concluded, it was Pitt who claimed that the complete handover of the French-controlled territory constituted an empire 'added to British rule'.

The end of the war very likely caused the Hudson's Bay Company men to believe that they would have free rein throughout the hunting grounds. This misguided impression, along with their 'long sleep' approach to business, was to prove to be their downfall in the short term. Soon, the old *coureurs de bois* re-emerged as new, even more adventurous fur trappers and traders. In their search for furs, they were prepared to venture further and further westwards in their Montreal canoes, as the beaver died off on the waterways of the St Lawrence.

Métis hunters were able to roam freely through the distant waterways. They were truly independent travellers, using bushcraft to survive, and living in very much the same way as their fellow traders, the First Nations people, with whom they dealt. Their skills, many of which were handed down through generations of intermarriage between the

First Nations and the French *voyageurs*, allowed them to be much more mobile than their competitors. They were required to trap the animals even in the winter months, which meant getting across the frozen rivers and lakes. Like their First Nations forebears, they lived a truly seasonal life, defined by the natural life cycle of the beaver, and at the mercy of the weather itself. But they were well schooled in the skills they needed to succeed and survive.

PAUL KANE

We know a lot about the *voyageurs'* way of life through the visual records of artist Paul Kane (1810–1871). I've used his drawings and paintings a lot in my own work and you can see his sketches throughout this book. The staggeringly accurate details of *voyageur* life portrayed in his artwork are second to none, and form the basis of much of what we now know about the beaver hunters and traders. Kane was one of those men who showed an enormous sympathy for the world he inhabited. He carefully studied what was around him, looked at everything with a fresh eye, and learned from what he saw. I discovered many tools of my trade through close study of his paintings and sketches, such as how to build an authentic traditional campfire, and how to hook a fishing line in Métis fashion. Kane is another one of those 'rocks in the river' that I've talked about before.

Paul Kane was born in 1810. His father, who was from Lancashire, had served in the Royal Horse Artillery before he took his family – Kane had seven brothers and sisters – to settle in Ireland. Some time between 1819 and 1822, the family emigrated to Upper Canada and settled in Toronto. Kane began his painting career as an itinerant portrait painter in the American Mid-West, before he went to Europe to learn from the paintings on display in Italy, France and England. While in London, he met the American painter George Catlin, who was trying to interest people in documenting the way of life of the native cultures in North America. Kane liked what he heard and returned to Toronto, via Alabama, after an absence of nearly 11 years.

oogemah-wah-be-gee *Young Swan*

Mrs. mesk

Kane received the support of the HBC's Governor, George Simpson, and in May 1846, he set off to join a canoe brigade heading west. He travelled on horseback with the Métis, witnessing a buffalo hunt first hand; he walked over the Canadian Rockies through the Athabasca Pass in snowshoes, and canoed down the Columbia River. In October 1848, Kane returned home – two and a half years after setting out. On his return, he recorded in his *journal* that 'the greatest hardship that I had to endure was the difficulty in trying to sleep in a civilised bed.'

He had made hundreds of sketches and from these he was able to paint 100 magnificent oil paintings, commissioned by a new patron – George William Allan – for the sum of $20,000. This enabled him to live as a professional artist at last. Some of his paintings were sent to London to be shown to Queen Victoria. He travelled to London and published a book, with lithographs of his paintings and sketches, but his dedication to Allan upset George Simpson, who broke off contact with him. Paul Kane died in 1871, but his paintings and sketches are an important part of Canadian heritage and I needed no encouragement to go and see them at the Royal Ontario Museum, where they are all collected.

The main reason his pictures and sketches fascinate me is because they are one of the best sources of information about the fur trade. According to the museum's curator, Ken Lister, Paul Kane travelled across the country specifically to document the people and landscape. As he went, he took every opportunity to sketch, using the HBC brigade stops and frequent portages to note down the detail of the surroundings and the people. The bushcraft he recorded was invaluable, and mainly because of their remarkable accuracy. I can take a Paul Kane sketch and make whatever object he's drawn, simply because the detail is so fine and so precise.

'He really felt, as he was going across, that he was making a document of the native people he saw and the Canadian landscape,' said Ken Lister. 'But he was also astute about the fact that these were going to be inspirational points for him – so that when he comes back and he's sat in his studio, he's going to have 600 sketches that he can take inspiration

Using spruce resin to repair a birch-bark canoe.

Lining a Montreal canoe.

Montreal Canoes could carry up to fourteen men and four tons of cargo.

The French River was a major trade route for *coureurs de bois*.

The charter by which Charles II gave land amounting to 40 per cent of modern-day Canada to the Hudson's Bay Company.

The much-sought-after beaver pelt.

Prince of Wales Fort was established by the Hudson's Bay Company in the early part of the 18th century to control the fur trade along the Churchill River.

Birch bark is the most amazing material. To make a container with it, first you have to scrape the reverse side carefully (1), then you can start to cut and fold it into the desired shape (2). Sewing it together is not easy – especially when your fingers are cold (3). Thin sapling bound round the edges creates a neat top rim. To make the container waterproof, I sealed the joins with a mixture of spruce resin and charcoal heated over a fire (4, 5, 6, 7). Attention to detail is an essential ingredient in successful bushcraft.

This recreation of an original trading post at Fort Carlton on the North Saskatchewan River shows a selection of the kind of goods that would be traded for furs.

from, to make his record. We have to keep in mind that it was the oil paintings that he saw as his record. The sketches were like field notes, for reference. The oil paintings are what he wanted to be known by.'

One of my favourite sketches shows blankets being dried in the sun. It looks as though the party has stopped after a rainstorm, draping blankets on bushes, above their tents, and by the fire. There is a beautiful tripod made using paddles as well as sticks, to hold it upright. The detail is staggering, and it inspires much of how I approach my own work in the wild.

'You can look at some sketches and he makes an almost direct transfer from sketch to oil, but you can look at others and the changes are quite dramatic,' said Ken Lister. He showed me a sketch labelled *Buffalo Pound Chute*, and explained: 'It's really a very accurate rendition of the way in which the Cree Indians made a buffalo pound, where you have these stumps which lead the buffalo into the pound. But there's a turn, so the buffalo are essentially tricked into running into the pound. But when you look at the painting itself, Paul Kane shows the stumps leading *directly* into the pound, which did not happen. So we have to know how to interpret his work, because if we're looking at the oil painting as an ethnographic document, we have to be able to ferret out of that those details in the painting – what is accurate and what is artistic.'

Kane's work and, in particular, his field sketches, are still considered a rich source of original material for students to gain insight into the country's past. Although he heavily reworked the oil paintings that he completed in his studio, bringing a greater sense of drama, perhaps, as well as an artistic sensibility to the paintings, they still contain a wealth of detail to ponder and absorb. Because the Royal Ontario Museum has both the paintings and his sketches, it's an invaluable place to study his work.

When I went back out on to the river, I felt his eye watching my work as I made my camp and set up my fire. It had to be accurate, not just for me, but as an exact chronicle of the heritage of the land. I really wanted to show that the lifestyle lived by those men, all those years ago, still had meaning for us today. There are so many facets of their way of life that we still use today, and so many others we have to keep using so that they are not lost.

FAST FOOD

One aspect of the *voyageur* way of life that we can witness through Kane's artwork was the way they solved the problem of eating while travelling through a land that would not easily support them. Not surprisingly, they borrowed heavily from the methods of the First Nations people. To feed themselves on the run, the *voyageurs* lived on pemmican, which they carried with them in bags.

Pemmican was made of buffalo meat (or, indeed, any other available meat), which was cut into strips and then wind-dried before being pounded into powder. The powder was mixed with buffalo fat and local berries (which helped to prevent scurvy, as well as providing fibre), and then tightly packed into leather bags. Pemmican could be formed into balls and eaten straight out of the bag, or cooked into a porridge-like soup. If the *voyageurs* had access to a fire, they could also slice, flour and fry it for a substantial hot meal.

Pemmican was a useful food for the travellers, as it never seemed to spoil. Its flavour and consistency were not, however, to everyone's taste. In his book *The Fur Land* (1879), author H.M. Robinson described it thus: 'Take the scrapings from the driest outside corner of a very stale piece of cold roast beef, add to it lumps of rancid fat, then garnish all with long human hairs and short hairs of dogs and oxen and you have a fair imitation of common pemmican.'

It doesn't sound very appealing.

HUDSON'S BAY COMPANY VS THE NORTH WEST COMPANY

The hardy *voyageurs* went on to form a loose alliance with some Scots and English merchants who had travelled across the Atlantic to become fur traders in Montreal. In 1783, they established the North West Company, in direct opposition to the HBC's monopoly. Known as Nor'Westers, the NWC men were more obviously entrepreneurial than the 'company' men of the HBC. They had, however, reckoned without one critical advantage held by the HBC men, who became known as the Baymen.

Although the Nor'Westers travelled deep into fur country, burned the Baymen's canoes, and established themselves to the point that the company controlled 78 per cent of the Canadian fur trade by 1800, they had reckoned without HBC's trump card. The HBC was run by such powerful people that it had the support of the Bank of England itself, giving it huge amounts of the finest credit available. And in a trade war, this was crucial.

Undercutting prices was an indisputably powerful weapon and the Baymen were always able to offer their buyers the lowest prices, using the money at their disposal to bribe the fur traders and drive the Nor'Westers out of business. While the Baymen may have lacked their predecessors' sense of adventure, they were commercially ruthless.

For four decades the two companies duelled through the

backwaters and rivers of Canada. The HBC directors' policy of passivity, where they waited for traders to bring the furs to them, was exchanged for a more expansionist role. Employees were despatched out to the west, to establish trading posts in the further reaches of the Company's territory. And as the Nor'Westers encroached on their land, the trade war often resulted in physical conflict.

Some of the differences between the Nor'Westers and the Baymen were the result of their ownership. The HBC was owned and run from London, by men who knew little about the life of a fur trader and had never set foot in the territory in which their money was made. The NWC was different. Not only were the owners based in the same country, but all of them were active in the business – indeed, many of them had travelled into the interior and traded there.

The HBC was able to deal crushing economic blows to the NWC not only because of its ties to the Bank of England, but also because they were able to realise a profit on their goods in a much shorter space of time. The route out of Hudson Bay and across the Atlantic made an enormous and profitable difference to the business cycle of the company. Ships could make a return journey from one continent to the other, trading goods and returning laden with furs, in under six months. The NWC, however, had to contend with far greater distances to reach their markets. Not only did they face long internal journeys from Montreal to reach the Western reaches where the beaver were still sufficiently abundant, but they then had to return along the same pathways, which wasn't always possible within the same year.

So, the NWC furs returning east might be the previous year's and, even when they reached the port at Montreal, they still had to travel across the ocean to London, where they would be sold. Only then would payment be made to the merchants, and this could be as long as three years after the furs had first been traded – for goods that had been paid for long ago. All in all, it is easy to see the enormous advantages that the HBC had over its competitor.

But this didn't stop the Nor'Westers from continuing to do business. Even though the greater distances they had to cover ate into their profit margins, they still forged deeper and deeper into the western reaches. Things finally came to a head between the two companies when the HBC interfered with the Nor'Westers' business in the Red River Valley.

The Métis who lived in the valley had established farms that mass-produced pemmican, which they then sold to the NWC for use by their *voyageurs*. The HBC 'sold' this land to a Scottish settler, Alexander Selkirk, who wanted to establish smallholdings for Scots turned out of their own homes by the Highland Clearances. The two groups, naturally, did not see eye to eye, as the Métis thought the invaders wanted to stop them supplying pemmican to the NWC and make them sell it instead to the new immigrants who had not yet found ways to live off the land. And this was, indeed, the case.

The Governor of the region was an American, Robert Semple. In June 1816, in a place called Seven Oaks (now in the modern city of Winnipeg), he and a group of men stopped a band of Métis led by a man called Cuthbert

Grant, who had seized a supply of pemmican to sell to the Nor'Westers. It's not clear who pulled the trigger first, but at the end of a ferocious encounter, Semple and 21 of his men were dead.

The massacre at Seven Oaks was a turning point. The Nor'westers could barely sustain the economic war they'd been fighting, and the deaths of so many people – over dried buffalo meat – sealed their desire to find an end to the fight. Discussions about a merger were held and, finally, a few years later, a new company was born. Both of the original companies were valued equally, at £200,000 each. The new company retained the name of the HBC, and now commanded a vast stretch of land. But even though the companies were merged, it was HBC that was pronounced the victor. In a funny sort of way, history gained retribution. In the last years of the 20th century, when the HBC sold off a portion of its retail businesses, the new business returned to the old name, and the North West Company was reborn.

A WORLD POWER

The new HBC company now controlled about a twelfth of
the earth's land surface – an area that stretched from the
Arctic Ocean as far south as northern California, and from
the St Lawrence basin across to the Pacific. At its height, the
Holy Roman Empire managed to acquire only a tenth of this
amount of land. And all of this was managed by no more
than about 3,000 personnel. It's small wonder that the HBC
not only issued its own currency, but also tried to use its
own calendar as well. While no one could claim that its
power was corrupt, the HBC most certainly had influence,
and it was able to dictate its own terms in whatever market
it entered.

Gradually, however, the concept of this vast company
holding such a firm monopoly began to fall out of favour.
Apart from anything else, the beaver population began to
decline. By 1854, in London alone some 509,000 pelts had
been auctioned off. These are the official figures; chances

are that pelts turned into coats and hats in Canada, and those smuggled home or given as gifts, were never recorded. The end result was that millions of beaver died to feed the ruthless demands of the fur trade, and it was a situation that was simply unsustainable.

What's more, the HBC's monopoly began to be undermined when illegal fur traders finally had their day in court. A Métis trapper called Guillaume Sayer was put on trial in 1849 for illegal fur trading (illegal, that is, in the eyes of the HBC). Although the court found him guilty, he was given no fine or any other kind of punishment, and set free instead. Misunderstanding – perhaps – the verdict, the hundreds of armed Métis waiting outside raised their arms in delight and shouted, '*Le commerce est libre! Le commerce est libre!*' – 'Trade is free! Trade is free!' As a result, the HBC could no longer count on their monopoly being upheld in court and, over the last years of the 19th century, their unique hold on the country of Canada faded.

The story of the Hudson's Bay Company is incredible in its own right but, perhaps more crucially, the company was

responsible for encouraging the exploration of Canada and the search for a trading route via the Northwest Passage. Three British explorers in particular stand out for their series of brave adventures, and each receives a more detailed telling of his story in the chapters that follow.

The HBC still exists today, making it possibly the oldest continuous commercial enterprise in the world. Its legacy is Canada itself. For me, however, there is another legacy

— one that is largely unremembered and unappreciated. That legacy appeared in the shape of an explorer who is little known here in the UK and, sadly, in Canada as well. Yet without him, so much of what the HBC achieved would have been impossible. Without his knowledge, understanding and voracious appetite for adventure, we would have only a limited picture of the First Nations' way of life in the 18th century, and little inkling of how they used the resources of the land to survive. This explorer's ability to document early bushcraft, and to adapt his lifestyle according to the wisdom of the native population, allowed whole generations of settlers and traders alike to survive what could be a very hostile land.

Who is this man? I'm speaking of Samuel Hearne, who is, for me, one of the greatest unsung explorers ever to emerge from Britain.

CHAPTER 4

SAMUEL HEARNE: NORTH OF SUMMER

Somewhere on the western edge of Hudson Bay, way above the 55th parallel, is a small inlet known as Sloop's Cove, formed when the ice sheets that once covered the land retreated at the end of the last ice age. It's a bleak, windswept place, the ground covered by a scattering of small scrub bushes. The soil is too shallow to allow much more growth, which would in any case be halted by the permafrost. Here, the temperature can drop below minus 30 degrees Celsius in winter, which is inhospitable by anyone's standards.

Since the end of the ice age, the land has been rising at the rate of about a metre every hundred years or so, and what was once a place deep in water is now dry land. It's no longer a mooring point for ships that have made the long crossing from Europe. Evidence remains of their stopovers there, with heavy iron rings set into the rocks for the sloops to tie up. There are also names handsomely carved into the rocks by the sailors who came ashore. Among those names – Robert Smith, George Holt and many others – is the name of the man who I consider not just one of the finest explorers of the far North, but one of the finest explorers ever to emerge from the British Isles.

Samuel Hearne signed and dated his name – 1st July 1767 – when he was 22 years old, and already a veteran of the Royal Navy, which he had joined at the age of 12. His story is one of extraordinary foresight and courage; of a determination to use logic to defeat problems he confronted; of a dirty lump of metal; and of sadness and cruelty.

His is a name that I kept coming across in my studies of bushcraft; there'd be a reference to him in descriptions of how people prepared animal skins for clothing, for example.

Or field guides would cite his work when laying out the medicinal uses of different leaves. Anthropologists would quote chapter and verse from his works, discussing how people used to live in this part of the world. In my study and appreciation of the northern wilderness, Samuel Hearne has become my tutor in so many ways.

Moreover, he has brought to life the traditions of the First Nations people, drawing on their knowledge and skills to provide a guide to survival in the seemingly harsh landscape of the north. Samuel Hearne was not just an explorer who travelled right across the northern part of this country and kept a *Journal* of his travels there. He was also someone who embraced and respected the skills and customs he uncovered and learned en route. He lived amongst the local people, and it was their heritage that he passed on to Europeans, thus ensuring their ability to travel and live on this land alongside its native inhabitants. So influential and inspirational was Hearne that he even attracted the interest of Samuel Taylor Coleridge, and may have inspired him to write his epic poem *The Rime of the Ancient Mariner*.

Hearne is, to my mind, more than a capable and extraordinary man, and his book, *A Journey to the Northern Ocean*, published in 1795, has been an invaluable guide for me, and an astonishing resource for my journeys into the northern wilderness.

THE BEGINNING OF GENIUS

Hearne's father died in 1748, only three years after Samuel was born. Widowed and with a daughter to bring up as well, Mrs Hearne took both her children to Dorset and it was from there that Hearne joined the Navy and took a position as servant to Captain Hood. He was no more than 11 or 12 years old. Nowadays this might seem grim, but such a fate was a pretty ordinary one for a boy of those times. After a few years in the Navy, he was fighting against the French in the Seven Years' War that ended – at least in Canada – with Britain's victory over her perennial enemy. During that war Hearne served under Captain Hood, clearly a tremendously able man from whom Hearne was to learn much. Admiral Nelson called Hood 'the greatest sea officer I ever knew'.

Later in his career, Hearne was able to put into practice lessons he learned about nutrition, navigation and medicine while in the Royal Navy. Instilled in him at such a tender age, those lessons likely stayed with him for his entire life.

What's more, the self-discipline he exhibited throughout the most trying situations could only have been possible in someone who had been carefully schooled in handling privation. Members of the Royal Navy were expected to be self-reliant, and Hearne displayed this trait to the highest order.

While he was serving in the Navy, many advances in navigation and medicine were made, including the use of a watch in course-plotting and map-reading. He embraced the knowledge around him, and applied it practically to the world he came to explore. Britain was alive with the convictions and theories being published by men as diverse as mathematician and physicist Sir Isaac Newton (1642–1727) and Scottish philosopher, economist and historian David Hume (1711–1776) – something made possible in part by the establishment of the Royal Society in 1660. In the mid-18th century, people were outward-looking, and always searching for potential. Samuel Hearne epitomises these characteristics, to the extent that I feel he fully embodies an expression from the Epistles of Horace that was popular at that time – *sapere aude*, or 'dare to be wise'.

Once the war ended, Hearne needed a job, and where better to apply than the Hudson's Bay Company? I was privileged to read a letter he wrote to the governors – Hearne's first entry into the historical record, in which he acknowledged the 'great obligation that I lie under to this good Company, and shall always endeavour to behave in a manner becoming to one in my situation'. It's a most unprepossessing letter – almost a whisper in history – from the man who I believe had the greatest impact on the exploration of Canada.

PRINCE OF WALES FORT

Hearne arrived in Canada in 1767, on the shores of Sloop's Cove, taking up a post for his new employers at the nearby Prince of Wales Fort. Initially he worked on the *Success*, under 'a Mr Joseph Stephens, a man of the least merit I ever met', but he was then transferred to help look after the fort.

The Governor at that time was a man called Moses Norton, whom Hearne disliked. He later wrote very harshly about Norton, whom he called a 'selfish debauchee' (and much worse), but although Norton also came to dislike Hearne for personal reasons, he still appears to have placed a great deal of trust in the young man.

It's hard to imagine a more desolate and lonely place than the Prince of Wales Fort. Even last year when I travelled there, the gates couldn't be opened until June because of the snowdrifts blocking them. The cold throughout the winters would have been very hard to deal with; in the years before Hearne's arrival, they used four cartloads of wood a day to keep the fires burning. Cannonballs were placed in the fires and, once heated through, they were hung in the windows to circulate warm air around the rooms. Nevertheless, it was still so cold that the beer would freeze in its tankards.

Although the fort was the recipient of numerous goods sent through HBC channels, the men did make use of the local produce and customs. Spruce beer, for example, was a particular favourite, and Hearne described its manufacture in detail. A kettle full of water was crammed with 'small pine', and they were boiled until they turned yellow or the bark peeled. The liquid was strained and molasses was added to the brew and then boiled again. This mixture was mixed with some cold water in a cask, after which Hearne suggested that the maker should 'take a Gun with a small Quantity of Powder, and no Wad; fire into the Bunghole, it will set the Liquor a working; in about twenty-four Hours stop the Cask down, and the Liquor will be ready to drink.'

The Hudson's Bay Company had established the fort in the early part of the 18th century, when the company needed to control the fur trade operating along the Churchill River. When Samuel Hearne arrived, it had been standing there, in one form or another, for 60 years. Initially a log cabin built by HBC man James Knight, work began in 1731 to construct the large, metre-thick stone walls, in the European star shape that remains today. The site chosen was at Eskimo Point, the rocky northern peninsula commanding the entrance to the Churchill River, which was selected for its strategic location. Chief factor Richard Norton predicted the structure would take six or seven years to complete using four teams of oxen and 84 men, but in reality the fort took over 40 years to complete.

HARSH REALITIES

I don't think the wind ever stops blowing at this remote fort, which must have been draining for the people living there. The conditions inside the fort were also harsh: the extreme cold, the smoky quarters, incessant bugs and random violence undertaken in the name of discipline were day-to-day realities. Despite the discomfort, men would readily renew their contracts to stay on with the Company, because life at a Hudson's Bay post offered a chance for advancement, a place to live with fairly decent food, and a dependable wage, which was much preferable to the uncertain future and hardship back home in Europe.

Luckily for Hearne there were occasional visitors – one of them the eminent astronomer William Wales, who travelled to the fort to observe the transit of Venus from Tahiti on 3rd June 1769. Hudson Bay was subject to pack ice that limited the shipping season to just two months, which would begin after the June transit, so it was necessary for Wales to travel to the fort in 1768 and over-winter there. His presence and equipment allowed Hearne to improve his skills in surveying and map-making.

The fort had initially been established as a symbol of British power and a statement of intent. It was a trading post to deal with the trappers and hunters, including the Dene (Chipewyan) people, Inuit from the northwest coast of

Hudson Bay, and the Cree living north of the Nelson River. It was also a base for northern exploration, whaling, and the search for precious metals, and it had another purpose, too. Its solid construction was designed to make it a defensive point during the on-going conflicts with the French, and a refuge for the traders to hole up in if the French attacked. It was built to protect the Company's cargo ships and their Royal Navy escorts. In the event of war, ships' crews could be employed in the defence of the fort and the Company's holdings on Hudson Bay. This was to prove very important in Hearne's own future, some years later.

The same issues of excessive drinking and illegal fur trading that had occurred in other trading posts took place here, but the diet – of fresh fish, migratory birds, caribou meat, local berries and the vegetables they managed to eke out from their short growing season – kept the men healthy.

'Myself and People are as usual all in good health,' wrote Hearne, 'but that is no wonder since the pureness of the air and the wholesomeness of the Diet makes it the healthiest part in the known world and what is very extraordinary at this place some of us think we never grow any older.' Like all company men, life for Hearne would have revolved around the fort in those first few years.

THE SEARCH FOR COPPER

The HBC's charter included responsibilities for exploring and, in the spring of 1768, the Prince of Wales Fort received accounts from the northern Indians of a 'Great River', which produced specimens of copper. This discovery prompted Norton, the fort's governor, to travel to London personally to see the Governors' Committee. There he put his case for an expedition to be sent out to these unexplored and barren lands, to report back on the copper deposits, any indications of fur trade potential that far north, and to map the land. Following Governor Norton's appeal, the HBC agreed to allow and to finance such an expedition. Hearne's place in history was secured.

Hearne was reportedly surprised when he was told that

he was the one appointed to investigate the reports of copper ore. He began to work out how he could make this difficult and dangerous journey. No company man and, by extension, no European, had travelled out across the frozen tundra, away from the edge of the Bay and into the heart of the interior, so no one knew what, exactly, he might face. Characteristically, Hearne was buoyed up rather than cast down by this thought.

THE EXPEDITIONS

All journeys have a beginning; Hearne's great adventure, in the end, had three. To find the source of this important and valuable mine, he first set out with his companions on 6th November 1769. His party included two Englishmen, along with several natives, who had mainly been selected by Moses Norton. It was a significant moment, for it was the first time that the Hudson's Bay Company had a man capable of carrying out a survey heading out to explore the interior – an interior that was completely uncharted and unknown. In setting out to cross the barren lands, Hearne was, in effect, stepping off the map of the known world.

Norton saluted their departure with shots fired from seven of the cannon, which still rest on the battlements of the fort today. He expected the party to be away for two years, and said that he would warn the ships to keep a lookout for them on their return. The expedition, however, was a disaster, and Hearne found himself returning to the fort, 'to my own great mortification', only a few weeks later, on 11th December.

One of the main problems Hearne faced was finding food. The land around the edge of the bay was so wet and boggy that it was almost impossible to cross, except in winter, when the snow and frozen water made it passable. But setting out in the winter months meant that Hearne was unable to eat off the land. When I travelled to the region, there was a multitude of bird life, albeit well camouflaged; however, these were migratory birds and would have headed south for the winter when Hearne set out. Other wildlife would have moved into the woods for shelter.

Hearne had not yet learned and adopted the native skills necessary for survival in the frozen winter months, and although he was accompanied by some First Nations people, he struggled to find enough food. He also had considerable problems with leadership, because the native man selected to guide him across the treacherous land and into the safety of the woods was inexperienced.

As a result of these setbacks, Hearne resolved to handle things differently. His first expedition offered him the opportunity to observe the ways of the native people, and provided a spark that kindled his interest in working with them to achieve his aims. He was already starting to become a resourceful man-of-the-land, who would not flinch from the hardships these expeditions brought him.

Just over two months later, on 23rd February 1770, he set off again, this time without any white men. On his first journey, the native people had assumed that the two Englishmen accompanying Hearne were his servants, and accordingly ignored them, providing them with no food or assistance. Furthermore, Moses Norton had insisted that no women should accompany them on the expedition, but Hearne was beginning to believe that he should travel in the native way, bringing along women who would prove invaluable support to the explorers.

There was so much snow on the battlements of the fort that they couldn't fire the cannon to mark his departure, so Norton gathered everyone together to give Hearne three rousing cheers to send him on his way. The party set off in high spirits, but once again Hearne was foiled – this time by the guides on his expedition, who, once again, were inexperienced and inadequate. After travelling for some time, it became apparent that the guides did not know how to cross into the barren lands ahead of them, nor were they equipped to provide food for the group. Once again, the lack of food began to have a telling effect on them all, and even Hearne confessed to 'extreme pain' after eating nothing much more than 'a few cranberries, water, scraps of old leather, and burnt bones'.

Although deer was plentiful, they did not have the resources to carry heavy loads of meat, and lived an existence of virtual feast or famine. Hearne wrote:

> ... *the Indians killed as many as was necessary; but we were all so heavy laden that we could not possibly take much of the meat with us. This I soon perceived to be a great evil, which exposed us to such frequent inconveniences, that in the case of not killing any thing for three or four days together, we were in great want of provisions; we seldom, however, went to bed entirely supperless until the eighth of March; when though we had only walked about eight miles that morning, and expended all the remainder of the day in hunting, we could not produce a single thing at night, not even a partridge! ... This being the case, we prepared some*

hooks and lines ready to angle for fish,
as our tent was then by the side of a
lake belonging to the Seal River ... [we]
moved about five miles to the West ...
to a part of the lake that seemed more
commodious for fishing. ... angling for
fish under the ice in winter requires no
other process than cutting round holes in
the ice from one to two feet in diameter,
and letting down a baited hook, which
is always kept in motion, not only to
prevent the water from freezing so soon
as it would do if suffered to remain quite
still, but because it is found at the same
time to be a great means of alluring the
fish to the hole ...

The constant supply of fish encouraged Hearne's guide to
suggest that they stay put until the 'geese began to fly',
which usually takes place around the middle of May. Hearne

agreed with this plan, and they set up a more comfortable camp to wait until the arrival of spring.

After their long stay, and subsequent travels further into the now melting north, Hearne came to realise that he and his party had travelled too far to the east. They found themselves on the tundra, where the increasingly harsh weather made it difficult to operate. He wrote, 'I let the quadrant stand, in order to obtain the latitude more exactly by two altitudes; but, to my great mortification, while I was eating my dinner, a sudden gust of wind blew it down; and as the ground where it stood was very stoney, the bubble, the sight-vane, and vernier, were entirely broke to pieces, which rendered the instrument useless. In consequence of this misfortune, I resolved to return again to the Fort.'

On the return journey, he was robbed of his possessions by some strange Indians, who came into his tent, took what they wanted from him, and left him with only the necessities: a knife, a file, an awl (so that he could repair his shoes), a needle, a razor (Hearne was not too displeased as they took the blunt razor and left him the better one) and 'as much soap as I thought would be sufficient'. He was dismayed, however, to find that his native companions had done little to protect him. He discovered that they thought their guide was a 'man of little note', and believed 'he was so far from being able to protect us, that he was obliged to submit to nearly the same outrage himself'.

SAMUEL HEARNE MEETS MATONABBEE

Samuel Hearne had no intention of returning to the fort with his tail between his legs, and his true character – one of optimism, strength, resolve and determination – shone through as he set out for home. Despite being robbed, he woke the following morning and set off immediately, writing that this day 'was the easiest and most pleasant of any I had experienced since leaving the fort'.

Less weighed down by the paraphernalia that he'd initially believed necessary for the journey, Hearne was actually cheerful. He was beginning to understand that he needed to adopt the skills and techniques employed by the natives in order to achieve success. He returned to Prince of Wales Fort after travelling for nearly nine months, and although this journey was no more successful than the first, Hearne had learned a great deal, and, most importantly, he had also met the man who would eventually make his expedition a success: Matonabbee.

This native of the Dene people was, according to Hearne, 'the most sociable, kind and sensible Indian I had ever met with'. A few years older than Hearne, Matonabbee – who had spent an early part of his life living in the fort – not only spoke English, but he also shared Hearne's determination to reach the Coppermine River. In fact, Matonabbee offered his own services, pointing out not only the 'misconduct of my guides' but also the 'very plan we pursued, by the desire of the Governor, in not taking any omen with us on our journey'. And Matonabbee clearly had a plan of his own. He said:

When all the men are heavily laden,
they can neither hunt nor travel to any

considerable distance; and in case they
meet with success in hunting, who is
to carry the produce of their labour?
Women were made for labour; one of
them can carry, or haul, as much as two
men can do. They also pitch our tents,
make and mend our clothing, [and] keep
us warm at night.

Thanks in part to Matonabbee, Hearne's *Journal*s comprise one of the finest anthropological records I have ever seen. Academic anthropologists may disagree with me, but I think there's nothing that matches it. Not only is the account he gives gripping, but the detail he brings to his drawings as well as to his descriptions is incredibly accurate. Hearne was the first explorer to successfully employ local methods and technology to cross the continent in a meaningful way – in particular, taking women along as an intrinsic part of the expedition.

His story interests me not only because of his achievements, but also because of the way he went about them. He was tenacious, and completely open-minded about learning the skills and customs of the native people. This was a unique characteristic, as in those days the local people were still considered to be inferior to Europeans.

THE THIRD JOURNEY

Hearne's third journey started in acrimonious circumstances on 7th December 1770. Moses Norton tried to slip into the travelling party some of his 'own' Indians, but Hearne refused because he'd found them 'of so little use' in his previous journeys. Hearne's stance offended Moses Norton 'to such a degree that neither time nor absence could ever afterwards eradicate his dislike of me, so that at my return he used every means in his power to treat me ill, and to render my life unhappy.'

This journey would take Hearne from the edge of Hudson

Bay, through the last few wooded areas at the top of the boreal crown running from east to west, and then north across the iced-over lakes and frozen tundra of the barren lands, a vast plain lying beyond the reach of the forest.

The barren lands really are the harshest environment imaginable. At their edges and in small sheltered hollows, little copses of wind-blown coniferous trees provided a meagre kind of shelter; towards the west, thicker strands of dwarf spruce held their own against the howling gales and bone-numbing cold. These were trees that took 300 years to grow to a height of just 1.8 metres.

As Hearne travelled further north, the trees and low-lying scrub disappeared and the plain was broken up only by rocks, sprouting out of the spongy, lichen-filled ground. On my visit there, I realised that one of the features of this exposed landscape were these ever-undulating ridges that seem to go on forever; it felt as though I was walking across the surface of an ocean that had been frozen in time. It's almost like being at sea on the land; there was food here – we saw some lemmings running around – but the main impression is of oceanic bleakness.

What made the pivotal difference to Hearne's journey this time was Matonabbee's knowledge of this ground and the hardships they would face en route. Matonabbee, who had been to the Coppermine River before, had the perfect strategy. They would leave in the depths of winter, travelling across the snowy wastes leading out from the edge of the bay to reach the woods where they would find food. They would then journey west, up through the forest, until they reached the edge of the treeline. Their arrival here would coincide with the end of winter, and they would join the migratory animals (caribou, for example) on their journey from their winter homes to the summer grazing grounds in the north.

Following the vast herds of caribou – some of them as large as half a million animals – would give Hearne's party a near-constant supply of meat as they ventured into a land where almost no sustenance of any kind was to be found amongst the knee-high dwarf birch that covered the surface. Additionally, the hides from the animals would provide them with fresh furs and new leather moccasins, both vital when the cold weather was so debilitating. Shoe leather was, wrote Hearne in May 1771, often 'a very scarce article with us'. Although moose hide was the preferred shoe leather, the party was travelling away from moose country into caribou country, and would have to make use of the resources available.

Even though Matonabbee's plan elongated their journey, as they would be staying within the treeline, further west than Hearne had ever travelled before, it was ideally suited to the conditions. It would also ensure that they had a virtual larder full of caribou to accompany them on both the outward and return journeys.

WITH THE TLICHO

I often wonder if Hearne was unnerved at the prospect of setting out into the wilderness without any map at all. It was like a voyage into outer space, into the complete unknown.

He headed out with a blank piece of paper that he was obliged to fill with details of the rivers, forests, lakes and mountains he encountered. Moses Norton had provided him with an 'Elton's quadrant' to replace the one broken on his previous journey, but he had little else to chart his journey. You can see a map of his route on the contents page of this book. Even today, experts estimate that Hearne was never more than about 32 kilometres out on his judgement of distance, from what current mapping can show. This is an astonishing, phenomenal piece of navigation for its time.

I personally witnessed the enormity of the Canadian wilderness, flying over it at low level in a small float plane. It's hard to believe or even describe the epic scale of Hearne's journey, which took months to complete, with few navigational tools. By May 1771, he had reached Lake Clowey, which is now known as Lake Eileen, where he met the Tlicho tribe.

The same tribe, which Hearne called the Dogrib, still lives here today, on the edge of the treeline. Their way of life preserves many of the traditional skills that Hearne would have acquired and used in his travels. Like the Tlicho, Hearne would have used the fine, soft tips of pine-tree branches to make a warm floor covering in his tents. Each piece would have been carefully slid into place to create a tight carpet of soft needles, which would be changed every two days.

The Tlicho elders – such as a man called Eddie I met there – have always found the forest to be a good provider, and many of the tribesmen to this day don't like to purchase food when the forest can provide them with such incredible bounty. The Tlicho were a poor tribe, and Hearne says that their extreme poverty would not permit 'one half of them to purchase brass kettles from the Company; so that they are still under the necessity of continuing their original mode of boiling their victuals in large upright vessels made of birch-rind. As those vessels will not admit of being exposed to the fire, the Indians, to supply the defect, heat stones red-hot and put them into the water, which soon occasions it to boil.'

One of the 'victuals' that Hearne describes is caribou blood soup. He wrote:

The most remarkable dish among them
… is blood mixed with the half-digested
food that is found in the deer's stomach or
paunch, and boiled up with a sufficient
quantity of water, to make it of the
consistence of pease-pottage. Some fat
and scraps of tender flesh are also shred
small and boiled with it. To render this
dish more palatable, they have a method
of mixing the blood with the contents

of the stomach in the paunch itself, and hanging it up in the heat and smoke of the fire for several days; which puts the whole mass into a state of fermentation and gives it such an agreeable acid taste, that were it not for prejudice, it might be eaten by those who have the nicest palates.

Hearne clearly grew quite accustomed to the particulars of what must have appeared to be unusual eating habits. He wrote, 'when the deer feed on the fine white moss, the contents of the stomach is so much esteemed by them [the Tlicho], that I have often seen them sit around a deer where it was killed, and eat it warm out of the paunch.'

I tried some blood soup myself, and found it warming, although it needed some salt to make it more palatable. The Tlicho elder to whom I spoke said his family would all come over to eat it when he had some, as it was an extremely popular dish.

The Tlicho made use of everything around them in the

forest, not only to prevent wastage of any description, but often because of superstition. For example, Hearne described the manufacture of fishing nets thus:

> *When they make a new fishing-net, which is always composed of small thongs cut from raw deer-skins, they take a number of birds' bills and feet, and tie them, a little apart from each other, to the head and foot rope of the net, and at the four corners generally fasten some of the toes and jaws of the otters and jackashes. The birds' feet and bills made choice of on such occasions are generally those of the laughing goose, wavey (or white goose), gulls, loons and black-heads; and unless some or all of these be fastened to the net, they will not attempt to put it into the water, as they firmly believe it would not catch a single fish.*

Many traditional skills have survived in the Tlicho tribe, perhaps more so than in other First Nations communities. Because there was no gold or silver to lure prospectors and explorers to their part of the country, and because it was charted later than the southern-most reaches of Canada, they kept their traditional ways for much longer. Shelter from the trees was inadequate for European travellers and the waterways were fairly inaccessible to larger craft so the traders who followed Samuel Hearne into these lands never attempted to travel deep into their heart.

Until the 1960s, this area remained remote and largely isolated. Some new roads and other developments were built in the 1970s but they failed to change the ways of these people. There were no jobs for the native people so they continued to practise their traditional ways of hunting, fishing and trapping. They also continued to use their own language.

In the last few years, the search for mineral deposits has opened up the area more, 'with the need for the younger people to get involved in a wage economy', as John B. Zoe of the Tlicho government put it. However, the elders have tried to instil in their young people the idea that they should know who they are first – to understand their way of life, their culture, their language – no matter what new methods of living are brought to their culture. They believe that if they maintain their own culture while adapting to the modern world, they will be much stronger as a result – becoming, effectively, two peoples, with old and modern combined. It's an interesting idea, and I certainly wish them every success in achieving their goal.

THE ADVENT OF SPRING

As spring came to the northern reaches, some of the waterways were opened up. Hearne's party travelled as often as possible in birch-bark canoes, which were essential not just for hunting geese and fishing, but also for travelling across the tundra via rivers and small lakes.

The Tlicho were known for the construction of their

birch-bark canoes, which, 'though made of the same materials with the canoes of the Southern Indians, differ from them both in shape and construction; they are also much smaller and lighter'. Hearne pointed out that these natives were frequently obliged to carry their canoes for up to 240 kilometres at a time, without 'having occasion to put them into the water'.

He wrote: 'All the tools used by an Indian in building his canoe, as well as in making his snow-shoes, and every other kind of wood-work, consist of a hatchet, a knife, a file, and an awl; in the use of which they are so dextrous that every thing they make is executed with a neatness not to be excelled by the most expert mechanic, assisted with every tool he could wish.'

These were the types of skills that Hearne carefully observed and often implemented later on in his journey, and every tribe provided its own unique methods of doing things. These canoes are, I can confirm, unbelievably light and portable. I could hold one high up over my head with one hand. Hearne purchased one early on in his travels,

Hearne's signature on a rock at Sloop's Cove, near Prince of Wales Fort.

Portrait of Samuel Hearne, 1796.

This tent with a wood-burning stove inside is similar to the one Hearne would have used on his expeditions.

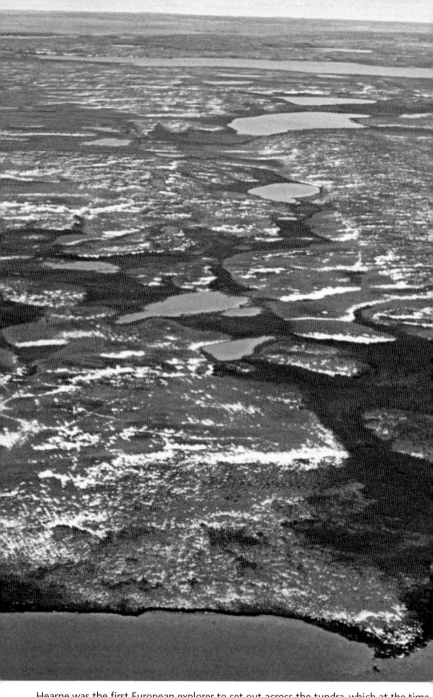

Hearne was the first European explorer to set out across the tundra, which at the time was totally unmapped.

Tlicho moccasins. Hearne preferred moose hide for his moccasins but had to make do with caribou as he got further north.

Above: Bloody Falls on the Coppermine River, where Hearne witnessed a massacre of Inuit people.

Right: The piece of copper he brought back with him that looks like a sleeping hare.

Every part of this beautifully carved totem pole on Meares Island has a significance. The moon and sun at the top symbolise the laws of the land, with the first law being 'respect' – respect for others and self-respect. The second symbol, the raven, represents 'all life' – in other words, respect for all life. The third symbol down is a mythical being, a double-headed sea monster. This represents a spiritual teaching about the balance of all things – facing your fears, facing yourself. The final symbol is the family crest, the wolf. This was always at the bottom, upholding all the laws above. We were told that having it on this level, accessible to anyone walking past the totem pole, meant it was there as a constant reminder of the laws.

for the princely sum of one knife – a clear illustration of the importance of metal tools in regions where they were scarce. This is also an indication of the fact that canoes were regarded, to some extent, as disposable objects. They could be discarded at the outset of winter, and then quickly remade the following spring, as part of what's known as the 'seasonal round'.

When Hearne and Matonabbee needed to build new canoes, they sent two men up ahead of them, taking a supply of wood. They'd found that if there was a dearth of mature trees further north, they might not find enough of the wood they needed. The canoes were often made on huge sandy banks by the sides of lakes, using resin and roots from the surrounding dwarf spruce trees. By the time Hearne and his men caught up, the canoes would be ready.

The advent of spring meant leaving behind the treeline and heading northwards into the barren lands, towards the Coppermine River. You can picture the scene: the men ahead, looking all the time for sources of meat, and the women behind, towing the poles, the tents and cooking pots along with the children. The weather was often unpredictable, and at a number of points in their crossing, the rain fell too heavily for them to light a fire, and they were forced to eat their meat raw.

Hearne noted, 'It often happened that we could not make a fire, so that we were obliged to eat the meat quite raw; which at first, in the article of fish particularly, was as little relished by my ... companions as myself.'

Even extreme necessity did not make the consumption of raw meat more appealing, but the travellers soon got used to it. Hearne said, 'By the time the weather permitted us to make a fire, we had nearly eat to the amount of one buffalo quite raw.'

TOWARDS 'BLOODY FALLS'

Hearne and his party were joined by various other people en route, and Hearne quickly discerned their objective: to attack and kill the Inuit they knew were camping alongside the Coppermine, at exactly the place that was Hearne's destination. The new arrivals were greatly intrigued by Hearne; they may have seen trade goods, but never the white-skinned Europeans who brought them to this country. When Hearne combed his hair, 'some or other of them never failed to ask for the hairs that came off, which they carefully wrapped up, saying, "When I see you again, you shall again see your hair".'

Hearne found himself entirely in the hands of this war party, and although they shared the same aim of reaching the river, they paid little attention to any of Hearne's views. At one point, Hearne was even concerned for his personal safety.

Leaving the women behind, the men of the party set off at pace, covering nearly 130 kilometres in four days, and they arrived at the Coppermine River on 14th July 1771. The war party was true to its word and immediately attacked the group of Inuit in a gory skirmish, at a place which Hearne later named 'Bloody Falls'. The party came towards the river, trapping the Inuit, and some 20 or so defenceless, naked people were roused from their sleep and massacred by the marauding band. Hearne described the event with clear consternation. He told of a young woman who ran from her attackers and curled herself around Hearne's legs before she, too, was brutally killed. Hearne saw that she was badly wounded and called for two men standing before him to finish her off. They simply laughed at him, and suggested that he must want an Inuit wife (which was considered to be a strong insult) to say such a thing. Hearne began to fear that he might be forced to end her misery himself, but the native people killed her as he stood over her. Hearne displayed great strength of character here; in the heat of battle, he was still prepared to stand up for what he believed in.

Hearne was also appalled by the treatment of the dead bodies and the destruction of virtually every item found there. The Inuit watching from the other side of the river could only stand and witness the bloodshed in horror. The Indians took their muskets and started shooting at them; the Inuit, who'd never seen guns before, rushed to look at the bits of lead squashed against the rocks – until one was hit in the leg, at which point they all took to their kayaks and paddled away. Many years later, when relating the incident in his *Journal*, Hearne wrote, 'Even at this hour I cannot reflect on the transactions of that horrid day without shedding tears'.

I had the opportunity to speak to an Inuit conservation officer at Bloody Falls, and he told me how he had been deeply shaken when he'd read about the appalling crimes perpetrated against his ancestors. There is, however, no animosity between these people today.

Allen Niptanatiak said, 'We've put all that behind us. You can't live in the past. Life is too short.'

In the local language, this place is not known as Bloody Falls, but 'Place of Large Rapids'. And it's certainly that – a dramatic, almost destructive place, where the river runs fiercely over the rapids and boils in swirls and pools. Allen Niptanatiak solemnly pointed out the spot where one of the locals – an old, near-blind woman, fishing off the rocks – had died when she was caught by the currents.

The local people often fish off the rocks, using spears known as kakuvak. These are a traditional tool most often used in winter fishing, and made of both wood and metal, which is abundant in the area. These spears were exactly the same sort that would have been used by the Inuit all those years ago.

Like many Canadians, Allen Niptanatiak held Samuel Hearne in high regard. He said, 'He opened up the north to the south, travelling by adapting the aboriginal methods and by taking them along as guides; he did a lot of great things for Canada.'

My own travels to the area were both onerous and exhausting, and it defies belief that Hearne was able to cover such huge, inhospitable distances on foot, and with a single native guide. Having made it to the ground and seen it for myself, my respect for this man is immeasurable. And I can confirm that Hearne really *was* here. Even the mud on my boots matches exactly the mud he described in his *Journal* – 'stiff, marly clay' – such was the detail that he provided.

FURTHER INTO THE NORTH

Hearne's party continued north and on 18th July 1771, they reached the Arctic, but found no evidence of a Northwest Passage. He wrote, 'This was no Northwest Passage, this was a rocky suburb of Hell.' Having been to this spot myself, I'm not sure that Hearne and his men ventured very far, as his description does not match what I found. I suspect that he climbed a hill and looked ahead, but made the decision to stop their journey there. I also think that Hearne and his party were probably slightly nervous; they had entered Inuit territory and, with 'Indians' in their party, they could be the subject of revenge attacks after the massacre at Bloody Falls. Apart from this, too, it was now July, and preparations had to be made to head back south before the cruel winter set in. It was an awfully long way home.

Of course, Hearne was still obliged to prove the existence – or otherwise – of a copper mine here, but when they reached the area, Hearne realised that the mine in question wasn't going to be an underground one, as he had expected. Instead, they found lumps of copper lying on the surface. They gathered up a few of these rocks to take back with them, and one of the specimens can still be seen today on show at the Natural History Museum in London. The copper rock is hare-shaped, and was mentioned specifically by Hearne in his *Journal*:

> *…The Indians imagine that every bit of copper they find resembles some object in nature; but by what I saw of the large piece, and some smaller ones which were found by my companions, it requires a great share of invention to make this out. I found that different people had different ideas on the subject, for the large piece of copper above mentioned had not been found long before it had twenty different names. One saying that it resembled this animal, and another that it represented a*

particular part of another; at last it was
generally allowed to resemble an Alpine
hare couchant: for my part, I must
confess that I could not see it had the
least resemblance to any thing to which
they compared it.

THE JOURNEY HOMEWARD

After they crossed Great Slave Lake, Hearne and his men
came across a young woman, alone in the woods. It turned
out she had been captured and had escaped some seven
months before, and had been living wild in the woods.
Hearne was incredibly impressed by her survival skills,
and by her ingenuity in adapting the methods she'd once
learned to the reality of her situation. She used rabbit furs
to make herself warm clothing, and, according to Hearne,
'supported herself very well by snaring partridges, rabbits
and squirrels; she had also killed two or three beaver, and

some porcupines. That she did not seem to have been in want is evident, as she had a small stock of provisions by her when she was discovered, and was in good health and condition.' He went on to describe her as 'one of the finest women, of a real Indian, that I have seen in any part of North America'.

This woman's story has become a part of the oral tradition of the Tlicho, and one of the elders told me that 'she made it back to her own people and was able to tell them about the fur trade, the guns and ammunition, about the forts and the houses that were there; so we describe her as the woman who discovered the Europeans, and her name according to the elders would be Whoneehcoo.' Her evident skill in surviving in this hostile land impressed Hearne, and he spent pages and pages describing her activities.

After several days in the woman's camp, the party trudged onwards, continuing their course homewards. By now, Hearne's feet were in agony, having been punctured by the sharp stones on which they walked. He wrote:

...the nails of my toes were bruised
to such a degree, that several of them
festered and dropped off. To add to this
mishap, the skin was entirely chafed
off from the tops of both my feet, and
between every toe; so that the sand
and gravel, which I could by no means
exclude, irritate the raw parts so much,
that for a whole day before we arrived at
the women's tents, I left the print of my
feet in blood almost at every step I took.
Several of the Indians began to complain
that their feet also were sore; but, on
examination, not one of them was the
twentieth part in so bad a state as mine.

Soldiering on after having his feet bathed and dressed by
the women, Hearne finally made it back to Prince of Wales
Fort on 30th June 1772. It was, he records, 'two years, seven
months and twenty-four days' (including the time spent on

his first two aborted expeditions).

No one has ever completed a journey quite like this. A round trip of 5,630 kilometres means that he had walked the equivalent of a straight line from Gibraltar to Moscow.

'I have the pleasure to think I have fully complied with the orders of my Masters,' he concluded modestly.

Hearne had achieved success in his expedition, opening up the northern wilderness to traders and settlers, but one of the most important aspects of his success had nothing at all to do with the Hudson's Bay Company. Hearne proved that by living from the land, as the First Nations people did, by trusting his life as well as the success of his mission to a native guide in the form of Matonabbee, and by adopting the habits, skills and beliefs of the people he met en route, he could travel this inhospitable land with relative ease. Rather than conquering it, Hearne set out to seek and respect its generous bounty, and this was one of the most crucial elements of his success. Almost every explorer who followed in his footsteps relied on his records, for he achieved something that no man had ever done before. Hearne was, in every sense of the word, a pioneer.

HEARNE'S LEGACY

There were other, wider-ranging results of his expeditions. For example, he 'put a final end to all disputes concerning a Northwest Passage through Hudson's Bay'. This was something upon which he did not dwell in the summary of his journey; instead, he focussed on the positive elements of his findings. For one thing, he had shown the unbelievable magnitude of the Company's territory. Before Samuel Hearne walked those thousands and thousands of kilometres, nobody had any exact idea of how wide the continent was, or how far north it extended. There was a common belief, for example, that the Pacific Ocean was just a little further away than the shores of the Atlantic. Hearne, however, not only showed that the country was vast – far larger than anticipated – but also that there was much, much more to discover. He developed friendships with the First Nations people, and a trust in their stories and words. He learned from them that there was a vast mountain range to the West – a barrier between the central plains, woods, rivers and lakes, and the ocean beyond. This type of knowledge was invaluable, and would lead to further HBC-funded expeditions into the Canadian wilderness – expeditions that would one day open up Canada completely.

Hearne's meetings with the native people, and his observations in his *Journal*, provide an unusual, authentic and completely original record of the land and its people. Two sections in his *Journal* are entitled, respectively, 'The Landscape and its People' and 'An Account of Flora and Fauna', making his account much more than a travelogue, or a businesslike description of the routes he took. He writes with passion and sincerity, and nothing is too small to escape his notice. It is this attention to detail that sets him apart from the other explorers of that time – and, indeed, beyond.

Perhaps the greatest achievement of his journey was his

methodology. Samuel Hearne successfully proved that the only way for Europeans to travel across the land was to use local knowledge. After Hearne, all of the great explorers of Canada were to follow his example.

CUMBERLAND HOUSE

Hearne's career didn't end with his journey into the northwest. In 1773, he was chosen by the Hudson's Bay Company to explore further west. The factors had become aware that canoes were coming back from the western parts of HBC territory, laden with furs destined for the North West Company's merchants. Furthermore, some of the furs that should have ended up in HBC hands were instead being intercepted by the enterprising NWC traders, and diverted east to Montreal.

To find out what was going on in western reaches of the country, the HBC despatched Hearne and 10 companions (eight Europeans and two Cree Indians) along the Nelson

River, through Lake Winnipeg and onto the Saskatchewan River. It was a journey covering about 725 kilometres – or about 40 days' paddling time.

Just two days into the journey, Hearne decided they were carrying far too many goods, including two 'pecks' of oats, and almost four kilograms of biscuits, and sent it all back home. He'd survived once before using the bounty of the land, and was sure he could do so again. He preferred to travel light.

At their destination, Hearne consulted with local chiefs and, in 1774, established Cumberland House. This trading post was built on an island already used by the Indian hunters, making it easily visible to those passing. It was an obvious trading point, and Hearne believed that it would encourage trade back into the hands of the HBC. Although Hearne did not know it, the waterways he was on continued to the Rocky Mountains – that mythical range that the native people had described so well. As Hearne set about constructing Cumberland House, he witnessed independent traders – the *coureurs de bois* – travelling past in their long canoes, which then returned heavily laden with furs. Stuck on the island overseeing the development of the trading post, Hearne and his men soon struggled for food and fuel, as the area was stripped bare. To set a good example, Hearne ate exactly what his men ate, and they worked together to find food for their survival, spending the whole of every other day checking fishing nets and foraging.

In his letters back to the HBC, Hearne spelled out the necessity for longer and larger canoes. He even tried to get some bigger canoes made, but was unable to find a craftsman prepared or equipped to take on the job. It is all very well having a trading post set this far out in the wilderness, Hearne wrote, but they needed to be mobile. They were not, he pointed out again and again, the only people transporting furs from the West.

The following year Hearne travelled east with 32 canoes, carrying the first loads of furs back to York Factory. He arrived with a multitude of suggestions for making Cumberland House a success, and ensuring that the HBC acquired the western trade. But while they took on board some of his advice, the Hudson's Bay Company decided against allowing Hearne to travel deeper into the western waterways. Instead, in 1776, Hearne was promoted again. This time he was put in charge of Prince of Wales Fort.

THE FRENCH ATTACK

Hearne's time as governor of Prince of Wales Fort was not a notable success. He had been bitten by wanderlust and he loved to explore, travel, meet faraway people, and eke out survival in hostile territories. The cold, dreary atmosphere of this huge stone fort failed to satisfy him, and it's unlikely that he gave the job the attention it required.

His personal circumstances had changed, too. Hearne had taken what was generally referred to as a 'country wife', although, being Hearne, he had a rather different approach to the situation than his fellow men. Most of his men had taken Indian women as their 'country wives', returning home to their own 'legal' wives when their time at the HBC

drew to a close. However, Hearne had chosen Mary Norton, the daughter of the previous governor, as his wife, and it is abundantly clear from his notes that he loved her dearly. He wrote:

She would have shone with superior lustre
in any other country ... none ever had
greater pretensions to greater esteem and

> *regard, while her benevolence, humanity*
> *and scrupulous adherence to truth and*
> *honesty would have done honour to the*
> *most enlightened and devout Christian.*

Along with his new love, Hearne threw himself into life at the fort. As governor, he set out to make changes in the living conditions, and proved that by proper attention to cleanliness and ensuring reasonable exercise, illness could be kept to a minimum. He also designed a skiff to replace the birch-bark canoes. These were to be prefabricated in London, be light enough for two men to carry, and sturdy enough to carry a ton of freight. Despite objections from many others, the Home Office backed Hearne's idea and the first skiffs were shipped to Hudson Bay in 1777. These were the beginnings of the famous York boats (see page 76), which eventually supplanted the bigger canoes.

But life in the northern wilderness was never easy, and the wheel of fate was about to take a tragic turn. The idyll came to an end on 8th August 1782, when three French ships under the Comte de Lapérouse arrived at the fort. The French Navy had been defeated by the British in the Caribbean, but these three ships had escaped north and were under instructions to enter Hudson Bay and take the forts. The ships came into view under a British flag, but Hearne was no fool and his Navy training had set him in good stead. He knew immediately that these were enemy vessels, and immediately halted the celebrations of his men, who were longing for contact with their homeland.

Hearne was aware that theirs was a perilous situation. Despite its huge stone walls, the fort was not well placed to defend itself against a disciplined and well-armed enemy. There was no source of water inside the fort should they be laid to siege and while the walls were thick, they were not high enough to give the defenders protection against incoming cannon fire.

Perhaps more importantly, Hearne had fewer than 40 men under his command, most of them untrained fur traders who would stand little chance against nearly 300 trained French sailors. Reluctantly, Hearne surrendered the fort without firing a shot. It was a sensible decision, of course, but one that would later be used against him, particularly by those men he'd antagonised over the years.

The guns at the fort are still broken from that catastrophic day, and when I visited the site, I could see clearly where the French had knocked the trunnions off some guns, and spiked others. They set fire to what could be burned, and blew up what they could destroy; and that was really the end of Prince of Wales Fort.

In those days, captured booty was considered to be the spoils of war, and the French would have ransacked the fort for anything they could eat, steal or burn. Lapérouse was shown Samuel Hearne's manuscript of his journey to the Coppermine River, but rather than turning it into a firelighter, he summoned Hearne and told him that whatever else he did, he must make sure that his work was published. It's hard to believe that this act of kindness and foresight really occurred, given the brutality of the invasion, and this gesture not only saved Hearne's irreplaceable record for future generations, but also confirmed its value.

Hearne agreed to help the French find a safe over-wintering spot for their ships, in return for being given a sloop and being allowed to sail back to England. He decided to leave his wife Mary behind because he thought she would be safest in the area she knew best, and where there were people to look after her. He had been very unsure that he would actually reach England without being thrown into a French prison, and didn't want her taken captive or harmed.

Imagine his horror and grief when he returned to the fort the following year to find that she had starved to death. She had been sheltered by her father for most of her life, and her rather pampered upbringing meant that she simply did not have the skills necessary to survive in such a place. She could have saved herself by taking another man to look after her, but such was her love for Hearne that she remained faithful to him.

She was very much the love of Hearne's life, and he was devastated by her death. He felt tremendous guilt about leaving her when he travelled to England, and never got over the fact that this decision may have cost her her life.

His grief was compounded by the death of Matonabbee, who had hung himself when he returned to the fort and found Hearne gone. His six wives and four children had also died of starvation that winter.

Hearne never recovered from the deaths of his beloved Mary and his good friend Matonabbee. From that time on, he determined to ensure that every child raised at trading posts in the HBC should be taught to live like locals, and schooled in the Indian way of life – learning skills that would have saved Mary's life if she'd known them.

LIFE GOES ON

Work had to continue at the new trading post on the Prince of Wales Fort site. Furs continued to come in from the woods, and decisions had to be made. But Hearne's heart was clearly no longer in it. Despite the obvious successes of his past, and the growing profitability of the new trading post, Samuel succumbed to intense melancholy. He was a man of action, and wanted nothing more than to leave the place where he had lost his wife and his best friend. The best medicine for him would have been a challenge – an expedition into the interior, to establish another trading post further west, perhaps – but the committee men of the Hudson's Bay Company didn't comply. They kept him at the fort, partly because he was good at his job, despite his unwillingness, but also because they had no understanding of his plight. Eventually Hearne retired due to ill health and returned to London in August 1787. With the aid of

old friends like William Wales, he set about trying to get his *Journal* published, then at the age of just 47, he died in London.

Hearne's *Journal* is a remarkable book and an extraordinary document; it's a book that does not just encourage re-reading, but one that repays the reader a thousand times over with every read. For Samuel Hearne does not just paint a thrilling and intricate picture of life in an unknown world; he provides a guide to living *safely*, and surviving anything and everything that nature could muster against him.

His story is that of one of the greatest explorers, naturalists and anthropologists who ever set foot on earth – it's the story of a man who set the template for all others to follow. His legacy is more than an amazing book, however; his monument is the vast northern wilderness of Canada. He was the first European to truly grasp the magnitude of this beautiful country because he'd walked so much of it. He pioneered the method by which this continent can truly be explored. I can say without hesitation that *all* of the most successful explorers that followed would use the methods that Hearne adopted from the native people, and adapted to his needs. In fact, I use many of them myself.

Hearne scratched his name into solid rock at Sloop's Cove in 1767; when I'm walking out in the immense world 'north of summer', I think it's possible to see his signature everywhere.

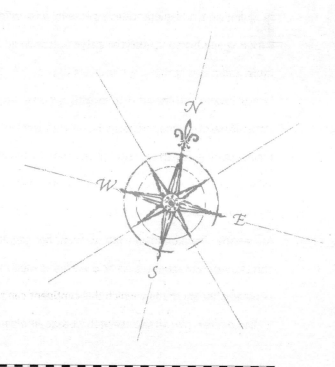

CHAPTER 5

IN SEARCH OF THE NORTHWEST PASSAGE

Much of the exploration of Canada's vast wilderness was sponsored by the companies controlling the fur trade, and it was in their best interests to push ever further into the north and the west to investigate new avenues of trade. The British and French governments were involved, too, searching for new routes from the Atlantic to the Pacific, and actively seeking bounty that would increase their coffers, and land that would increase their colonies. As Canada opened up from east to west, her geographical borders began to be established, and efforts were made to uncover what lay to the west of Hudson Bay.

The discovery of the Northwest Passage was becoming

an increasingly elusive goal. For centuries, its existence had been the subject of much conjecture, but explorer after explorer had failed to locate it. Some even died in the process. Several nations had sent sailors and explorers to the western Canadian shores to look for its mouth; inland, the large fur-trading organisations were encouraging their own explorers and navigators to search the areas north and to the east of Hudson Bay for the crossing. In the mid-18th century, the English parliament offered a reward of £20,000 for its discovery – a huge sum of money in those days, and enough to inspire countless expeditions into the wilderness.

Some of these explorers went on to become enormously important men in Canada's history, and their success was based largely on the skills and techniques established by Samuel Hearne. Alexander Mackenzie (1764–1820) and David Thompson (1770–1857) both journeyed using the methods that Hearne had found so productive – adopting the habits and lifestyles of the local inhabitants of the land and often travelling without any other European accompaniment. Their stories are fascinating, and their

expeditions opened up a rich new landscape and introduced them to some extraordinary indigenous people. Mackenzie and Thompson were responsible for blazing a trail across the Rocky Mountain ranges that Hearne had heard about, and reaching the vast sea that lay beyond. Their names are, therefore, just as important as Hearne's, and their successes equally vital to the development of Canada.

Unlike Hearne, who was, through and through, a Hudson's Bay Company man, Thompson and Mackenzie were both employed by the rival North West Company. Their explorations were not specifically aimed at reaching the Pacific, but that is what they eventually achieved. They were explorers and cartographers, set on finding the elusive Northwest Passage, and charting the unknown territories in order to establish greater and more diverse trading routes.

The Pacific coast was also the focus of expeditions from the west, and Captains James Cook (1728–1779) and George Vancouver (1757–1798) landed here, charting the islands and coastline in their search for the Passage, and initiating trade with the local people at Nootka Sound in 1774. With the Hudson's Bay and the North West Companies blazing the trail from the east, making their fortune from beaver pelts, other traders approached from the west and begin trading with First Nations people for goods that could be imported back to their homelands. The pelts of the sea otter, for example, sold for massive profits in Asia. And so it was that Canada's Pacific coast became a key trading post on round-the-world voyages to the Far East.

While the 18th-century and early 19th-century explorers may not have located the Northwest Passage, despite intensive efforts, these expeditions were not in vain. For a whole new world *was* opened up, and the magnificent bounty of the Pacific coastal region revealed.

A SCOTTISH FUR-TRADER

Alexander Mackenzie was born in Scotland in 1764, emigrating to New York with his parents at the age of 10. Four years later, he travelled to Montreal in the north, where he studied before becoming a clerk with fur merchants Finlay & Gregory. Five years later, he was offered a share in the company on the condition that he travelled to Grand Portage (near the present-day Grand Portage in Minnesota) to serve at the trading post there. Mackenzie was happy with this proposal, and keen to experience trade first hand.

Mackenzie's career was beginning just as the American Revolution drew to a close, and the Montreal merchants had started to cast their eyes westward, because the new Canadian-American border prevented expansion to the south. These merchants were ready to invest in an expedition

Red elderberries, which must be cooked before eating

There's an amazing diversity of fruit to be found on the Canadian Pacific coast. We found eleven varieties within the space of 100 metres – the richest plant food resource I've ever seen in Canada. Bears have a key role in this biodiversity, eating the berries and then re-distributing the seeds through their droppings.

The Western red cedar is a called the 'Tree of Life' on the Pacific coast of Canada. The wood is easily carved and the bark has many uses – for containers, mats, footwear, clothing and other essentials – so the trees are treated with great respect.

Stripping the bark doesn't damage the tree; it will continue to grow as long as this is done carefully.

A cedar with the bark strip removed. These trees are recognised as culturally modified, carrying the scar forever. This is accepted because it has been done with a purpose.

When the bark strip has been removed, it can be carefully formed into a package for easy transportation – a skill in itself.

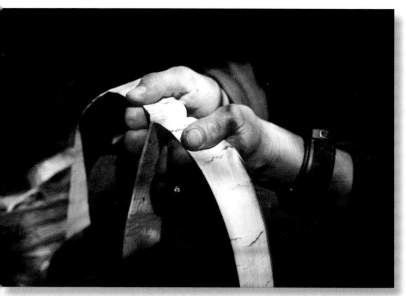

Taking off the outer layer reveals the softer inner bark, which is easier to work.

Thin strips are the perfect material to weave into a durable basket

John Rae's journey took him deep into polar bear country, as did mine.

The frame for these snowshoes was carved from an ash log
and they were bound with rawhide.

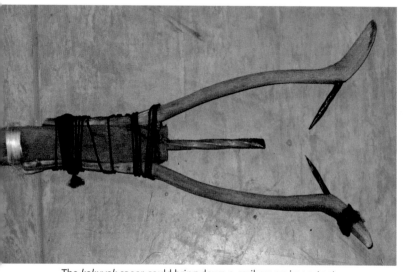

The *kakuvak* spear could bring down a caribou, an important
source of food for Rae and his men.

A masterclass in igloo building. A circle is drawn where the first ring will be laid (1). A harpoon is used to test the hardness of the snow, then blocks are cut out of the firmer snow below the surface (2).

As each row is laid, a snow knife is used to make the blocks sit neatly against each other (3–5). A final block is pulled into place at the apex (6) and you have a well-insulated shelter to provide protection from the elements.

A demonstration of throat singing by two Inuit girls.

that would uncover a commercial route to the Western Sea that Captain Cook had described. All that was left was to find a way to reach it by land, across the Canadian west.

From 1785 to 1787, MacKenzie traded furs for Finlay & Gregory, which had expanded to become Gregory, MacLeod and Company, at Lac Île-à-la-Crosse. In an effort to stem growing violence amongst rival trading companies, Gregory, MacLeod and Company merged with the North West Company, which actively sought to promote exploration in the pursuit of a fur-trading monopoly. Mackenzie was asked to spend the winter in Athabasca, and to ascertain whether the massive river to the north, which flowed out of Great Slave Lake, actually did go to Cook Inlet in Alaska, as Mackenzie's contemporary, explorer Peter Pond, believed.

Alexander Mackenzie's dream of finding a new way to the Arctic Ocean was not simply a corporate ambition. Some 20 years previously, Samuel Hearne had succeeded in reaching the Arctic Ocean by way of Lake Athapapuskow, travelling north-eastwards along the Coppermine River to the frozen sea. Through his fur-trading activities for the North West

Company, he had learned from the locals he encountered on his travels that there was a vast river to the north – as big as the Saskatchewan and the Churchill Rivers, the largest they had charted in the area – on which no white man had ever set eyes. The potential commercial benefits of finding this river, and adding his name to the growing list of great Canadian explorers inspired Mackenzie to begin his voyage to the north east.

In June 1789 he set out, recording in his diary: 'We embarked at nine in the morning at Fort Chipewyan, on the south side of the Lake of the Hills ... in a canoe made of birch-bark.'

THE GREAT RIVER

Mackenzie secured the services of a native guide known as the 'English chief', who was in many ways a natural successor to Hearne's indispensable guide Matonabbee. Mackenzie led the way in his own canoe, accompanied by four French-Canadians and a young German called John Steinbruck.

Mackenzie quickly identified the location of the so-called 'great river', and his expedition descended it (a distance of almost 7,000 kilometres) in just 14 days. He continued on to the Arctic Ocean, and stayed on Whale Island for four days. The discovery of this river, which was clearly one of the longest in the world, did not excite his employers. Because it did not provide a passage to the Pacific, it was of no immediate use to them. Mackenzie's frustration led him to call his great river 'Disappointment River', but it was later renamed the Mackenzie River in his honour.

Although this first trip had a positive impact in helping to map the northern regions of the continent, Mackenzie and the North West Company remained determined to find the 'Western Sea'. In 1791, Mackenzie returned to England to study new advances in the measurement of longitude, returning in 1792 to set out, once again, to find a route to the Pacific.

He was accompanied on his second expedition by native

guides, French *voyageurs*, and a dog called 'Our Dog', and he left Fort Fork to follow the route of the Peace River. When he got to the upper reaches of the Fraser River, he was warned by the First Nations people that the lower parts of the river were unnavigable and home to hostile tribes, so he altered his course to follow an established trading route through the West Road River, crossing over the Coast Mountains, and descending along the turbulent Bella Coola River. Two days later, he came upon six curious little huts built on stilts. He wrote, 'From these houses I could perceive the termination of the river, and its discharge into the narrow arm of the sea.'

The guidance of the native people had proved not only accurate but invaluable, and on the 20th of July 1793, Mackenzie reached the Pacific coast at Bella Coola, British Columbia, on an inlet of the Pacific Ocean known as North Bentinck Arm. Greeted by the affable nation of the Bella Coola, he labelled their settlement 'Friendly Village', and learned from them that he had missed the visit of explorer George Vancouver, an Englishman determined to find the Northwest Passage via the Pacific, by just six weeks.

He announced his arrival by using a vermillion and bear-grease mixture to paint a rock with the words:

Alexander Mackenzie, from Canada,
by land, the twenty-second of July, one
thousand seven hundred and ninety-three.

This rock, near the water's edge in Dean Channel, still bears the same words, which were permanently inscribed by surveyors. The site is now part of Sir Alexander Mackenzie Provincial Park.

Alexander McKenzie had completed the first recorded transcontinental crossing of North America to the north of Mexico, beating the venerated American explorers Meriwether Lewis and William Clark, who would not make it across to the Pacific for another 12 years.

Once he reached the ocean, Mackenzie's intention was to continue westward and out on to the open sea; however, the aggressive Heiltsuk people had started to make their presence felt, and he headed, instead, for home. His party reached Fort Chipewyan in a month, with every member of the crew alive and well. Although he had proved that it was a viable journey, it was considered to be too long, too expensive and too difficult for Montreal trade.

Mackenzie went on to form his own company – the XY Company – in 1798, which amalgamated with the North West Company in 1804. His account of the voyage was published in 1801, and offered an enormous contribution to the growing knowledge of the continent. In 1802, Alexander Mackenzie was knighted for his efforts, and he served in the Legislature of Lower Canada from 1804 to 1808. After gradually withdrawing from the fur trade, he finally returned to Scotland in 1812, where he married and fathered three children. He died in January 1820.

AN UNKNOWN WORLD

Without the guidance and wisdom of First Nations guides, it is unlikely that Sir Alexander Mackenzie would ever have achieved his goal of reaching the Western Sea. Adopting traditional methods of survival and travel, as Hearne had before him, Mackenzie was able easily to negotiate the hostile conditions he encountered, and adjust his route in accordance with the knowledge of the native people. Friendships were struck, and these were to stand him in good stead throughout his journey to and from the sea.

En route to his final destination, Mackenzie forged relations with various tribes – both shy and hostile – and recorded his activities in *Journals* that would be published a few years later. For a man who was only 28 years old, his observations are detailed and insightful, and presented later explorers and surveyors with vital information about the people of the regions crossed. Just north of the Horn Mountains, for example, he met with a shy and wary group of First Nations, and wrote:

> *There were five families, consisting of twenty-five or thirty persons, and of two different tribes, the Slave and Dog-Rib*

Indians. We made them smoke, though it
was evident they did not know the use of
tobacco; we likewise supplied them with
grog; but I am disposed to think that they
accepted our civilities rather from fear than
inclination. We acquired a more effectual
influence over them by the distribution
of knives, beads, awls, rings, gartering,
fire-steels, flints, and hatchets, so that
they became more familiar even than we
expected, for we could not keep them out
of our tents, though I did not observe that
they attempted to purloin anything.

Mackenzie described how they plied him with increasingly

fantastic stories about the river that he had set out to

explore, telling of horrifying monsters and evil spirits that

might be met if he continued in the same direction. He

took a pragmatic approach to this knowledge, gleaning

from it the information he needed to make decisions about

how they would progress, but also understanding that the superstitions and mythology of the First Nations often had a kernel of truth.

At other points in his journey, Mackenzie took the time to note down the intricacies of the flora and fauna, and took great pleasure in the discovery of animals, plants and birds that were unfamiliar to him. Whereas beavers had been a familiar sight along the rivers they travelled, they were introduced now to sea otters. Mackenzie wrote:

> *At about eight we got out of the river,*
> *which discharges itself by various*
> *channels into an arm of the sea. The*
> *tide was out, and had left a large space*
> *covered with sea-weed. The surrounding*
> *hills were involved in fog. The wind was*
> *at West, which was a-head of us, and*
> *very strong; the bay appearing to be from*
> *one to three miles in breadth. As we*
> *advanced along the land we saw a great*

number of sea-otters. We fired several
shots at them, but without any success
from the rapidity with which they plunge
under the water.

He was fascinated by the magnificent cedar trees – some of which he documented as being some seven metres around their girth, and tremendously high. These trees were, and still are, central to indigenous traditions; the lightweight, aromatic wood was necessary for the creation of totem poles and ocean-going canoes, and clothes and baskets were made from the bark. Following in the footsteps of some of these great explorers, I too was awestruck by the grandeur of the red cedar.

THE RED CEDAR

I met up with Joe Martin, a member of the Tla-o-qui-aht First Nation, and he told me about the history of the dugout canoe and the work involved in making one. The gigantic red cedar was the preferred wood. If possible, the highly esteemed builders in the communities looked for drift logs, but if these were unavailable, trees were felled using a stone maul with bone, antler or stone chisels and controlled burning. Hand adzes were used to shape the exterior form, after which the interior was hollowed out. Next, hot water was used to render the canoe pliable, and wooden spreaders were inserted between the gunwales to extend the beam of the canoe beyond the natural width of the log. High-end pieces were carved separately and attached to the bow or stern using a traditional sewing technique.

The indigenous people of the Western coast were renowned for their artwork, and each canoe was colourfully decorated with animal designs using red ochre, black charcoal and assorted animal teeth and shells. The canoes were manoeuvred by leaf-shaped or lanceolated single-blade paddles, and square cedar-mat sails. The skill with which the great trees were fashioned into functional floating sculptures – boats that were used for everything

from daily fishing to major voyages – became a hallmark of many tribal cultures.

Because they were designed to navigate the choppy Pacific waters, the canoes were sturdily built, with some reaching 24 metres in length. These massive ocean canoes, used for trade, whaling and sealing, were mistakenly referred to as 'war canoes' by settlers. Early maritime explorers recorded their observation of authentic war canoes, with a high and wide prow to shield the paddlers from enemy missiles. I can only imagine the sight that Cook, Vancouver and Mackenzie encountered when they first visited these waters, with all manner of marine life from shellfish to whales, seals and sea lions .

Mackenzie's description of his journey was the crucial inspiration behind the expeditions of another brave and intrepid young explorer, David Thompson, who followed immediately in his wake.

THE GREAT GEOGRAPHER

David Thompson (1770–1857) has been called 'the greatest land geographer ever' for his remarkable feat of mapping nearly five million square kilometres of North America by the age of 42. He is, in every sense of the word, just as important as Samuel Hearne in the history and development of Canada; however, the two men, who at one point worked together, could not have been more different.

Hearne was open to the world he inhabited, prepared to test any theory and any practice. No matter what their provenance – modern or traditional – he would choose what worked and hone the skills and information he acquired until it became its own. Thompson, however, was a different kettle of fish. While he did not baulk at experiencing hardship in the course of his journeys, he was a devoted Christian and firm in his beliefs. While he was perfectly content to adopt the practical skills of the First Nations, he often drew a line at taking on board their folk wisdom if it contradicted his own beliefs. His religious fervour brought him into conflict with Hearne, when the two men worked together at Churchill, south of the Prince of Wales Fort.

David Thompson was born Dafydd ap Thomas. His Welsh parents had recently moved to Westminster, Thompson's first home, and his father died when he was two. As a result of the family's hardship, he and his brother were placed at the Greycoat's School in central London. He was handpicked from here, at the request of the Hudson's Bay Company, which had a policy of recruiting bright young talent. Thompson wrote: 'It had been the custom for many years, when the governors of the factory required a clerk,

to send to the school in which I was educated to procure a Scholar who had a mathematical education to send out as Clerk, and, to save expenses, he was bound Apprentice to them for seven years.'

A few years ago, I had the great honour of unveiling a plaque at the very school that Thompson attended centuries ago, which had been laid in his honour. It was remarkable to consider that a pupil from an 18th-century central London school could have gone on to achieve so much, and as I later followed in his footsteps, making my way along rivers and paths, I saw exactly what a difficult undertaking his travel must have been.

Although his background was impoverished, Thompson had a rather privileged and very religious education, and his sheltered upbringing meant that he was unprepared for the harsh realities of life in the northern wilderness. While the committee men of the HBC instructed Hearne to treat Thompson gently, excusing him from harsh duties so that he could concentrate on becoming an administrator in the company, Hearne did quite the opposite, believing that he should toughen him up in preparation for life at the fort. He had no time for a pampered schoolboy, having entered the Navy at the age of 12, and he did not hesitate to put Thompson straight to work. He ignored the boy's religious fervour, and was even known to prevent him from attending Sunday services.

He did, however, set Thompson to work transcribing

some of his *Journals*, and the knowledge that Thompson would later accrue in his own work was based very much on Hearne's experiences.

A LUCKY ACCIDENT

Thompson grew to hate Hearne, and at the first opportunity left his employ to go west to Cumberland House. From Churchill, he travelled north to Manchester House where, the following winter, he fell and broke 'the large bone of my right leg'. His injury was, in fact, horrific, and the HBC employee who ran Manchester House at that time, William Tomison, ordered that Thompson be watched, 24 hours a day, for three weeks. Nearly five months later, Tomison wrote: 'David Thompson's leg I am afraid will turn out to be a mortification as the joint of his ankle has never lowered of the swelling.' Thompson limped for the rest of his life; however, his enforced period of inactivity gave him the opportunity to work under the HBC's surveyor, Philip

Turnor. Not only was his pleasure in mathematics rekindled, but he also expanded and enhanced his astronomical and surveying skills.

When his apprenticeship with the HBC came to an end, instead of accepting the customary suit of clothing that would normally have been granted, he wrote to the committee men with an altogether different demand: 'Your Honours specified in the terms of my indenture to give me at the expiration of my terms a complete suit of clothes, both linen and woollen. In lieu thereof shall be much obliged to your honours to let me have a brass sextant by Peter Dolland of not less than ten inches radius ...' His letter goes on with further specifications, and, in addition, he requested an artificial horizon device – 'a pair of parallel glasses', as well as a compass, thermometer, two watches, drawing instruments and the two-volume set of Robertson's *Elements of Navigation*.

Turnor was impressed with his young employee, and welcomed his wilful determination. He wrote a letter in support of Thompson, saying:

*In my Journal which contains
my observations I have had some
observations made by your Honours'
unfortunate apprentice David Thompson.
I am fully convinced that they are genuine
and should he ever recover his strength
far enough to be capable of undertaking
any expeditions, I think your Honours
may rely on his reports of the situation
of any place he may visit. Should he
not be capable of travelling he may be
very useful in giving others instructions
by which any of moderate abilities
may be made more capable of taking
observations than any have yet proved
which your Honours have sent out of
England.*

THE JOURNEYS BEGIN

By September 1792, David Thompson had recovered sufficiently from his injuries to be able to set out, on the company's behalf, for the area around Lake Athabasca, with the aim of setting up a trading post by the lake. Over the next few years he moved around the various trading posts in the waterways of the area before he was finally able to find the most direct route to the southern end of Lake Athabasca in the spring of 1796.

The following winter, Thompson decided to leave the Hudson's Bay Company for its greatest rival, the North West Company. This was an extraordinary thing to do, not least because he did not give notice and simply packed his bags and walked away. The reason he gave was that he wanted to focus on map-making, not trading furs. Working for the North West Company would allow him to advance deeper into unmapped territory without being expected to trade as he went.

What David Thompson achieved over the next few years is little short of astonishing. Before he settled near Montreal in 1812, he had travelled almost 89,000 kilometres – by canoe and on foot – across Canada and over the Rockies, traversing the Columbia River to the Pacific Ocean, and then making his way down into the United States.

Wherever he went, every day, without fail, he would note down the latitude and longitude of his position, the temperature, and some geographical information, enabling him to map the country accurately years later. Sometimes he even entered the magnetic inclination on his maps. His journal illustrated his multifaceted gifts as scientific explorer, geographer, cartographer and naturalist.

Some scholars have described his journal as one of the finest works in Canadian literature. His directness in prose, his modesty and ability to see himself and others, his sharp powers of observation and intense practicality all contribute to a vivid glimpse of early Canadian pioneering.

He grew to love 'the forest and the white water, the shadow and the silence, the evening fire, the stories and the singing and a high heart', and on his own initiative he explored, surveyed and mapped nearly half the continent.

Thompson's first expedition began at Grand Portage in August 1797. His initial trip took him along the length of the 49th parallel westward, mapping the NWC trading posts as he went. He continued through Lake Winnipeg and

up to the Red Deer and Assiniboine Rivers, which drained into Lake Winnipegosis and Lake Winnipeg respectively.

Later that year he travelled up the Souris River and over-wintered with the Mandan Indians, after which he ventured up the Red River and the Red Lakes River where he found himself at Turtle River Lake (in present-day Minnesota).

This was, he declared, the head of the great Mississippi River which eventually led into the Gulf some 4,000 kilometres south. In fact, he was out by only a few kilometres – the headwaters of 'Old Glory' have now been established just south of this point, in Lake Itaska – but it was still a remarkable discovery from one so young.

Thompson's next journey sent him further west, and in February 1798 he surveyed and completed a route that connected the far-flung parts of the NWC's trading territory as far away as the Red River with the company's main base at Grand Portage. Not content with that journey, he carried on north and reached Lesser Slave Lake in 1799.

That year, at Île-à-la-Crosse, he married Charlotte Small, about whom he later wrote: 'My lovely wife is of the blood of these [Cree] people, speaking their language, and well educated in the English language, which gives me a great advantage.' During their long life together – in which Thompson, unusually for the times, did not stray or take a 'white wife' – they had 13 children, although not all survived childhood.

Thompson continued to probe westwards and in the spring of 1800 he arrived at Rocky Mountain House (which remains the name of the thriving town built on that spot), where the plans for his attempt at crossing what seemed an impassable barrier to the Europeans were drawn up.

CROSSING THE ROCKY MOUNTAINS

The Rocky Mountains stretch almost 5,000 kilometres from northern Canada down to New Mexico, and not far to the north-west of Rocky Mountain House stood the highest point of the Canadian Rockies, Mount Robson, which rises to a height of nearly 4,000 metres.

Over the next couple of years Thompson made a number of attempts to cross the Rockies, and on almost every occasion he was forced to turn back, not always because of the conditions but also because of the bitter opposition of the Blackfoot, who thought that the Europeans had come to trade with their enemy, the Kootenay. They were worried that the Kootenay would be supplied with guns and they would lose their advantage over them. And they were right to be concerned, because Thompson and his men did do a little trading with the tribesmen initially, and opened up full-scale trading some time later.

In between his attempts to cross the Rockies, Thompson travelled up and down the Saskatchewan River basin, and in 1802, he followed the river network all the way down to Lake Superior. In 1803, Fort Kaministiquia on Lake Superior (later renamed Fort William, and now known as Thunder Bay) replaced Grand Portage as the North West Company's headquarters, and the following year Thompson was made a partner in the company. This gave him even more sway than before, and the other partners agreed that the company should be expanded west over the Rockies.

In these first few years of the new century Thompson

busied himself mapping the entire territory of the region east of the Rockies for the NWC. In the spring of 1807, Thompson – with his family and a disparate group accompanying him – made his trip across the Rockies, through Howse Pass, arriving on the Columbia River on 30th June. He and his party travelled along the Columbia for some time, often on foot, but here, his usually infallible navigation let him down. The Columbia took a turn and began to flow north, away from where Thompson expected it to flow, and so he decided that they were travelling on the wrong river. Deflated, he went no further, and when the colder months arrived, he and his party over-wintered in Kootenae House, a trading post at the southern end of Lake Windermere, from where they traded with the Kootenay for supplies.

Thompson continued his surveying, travelling down into the area of the northern US states of Montana and Idaho, where two more NWC trading posts were established. However the Blackfoot put an end to his journeys for a time, refusing to allow the men to trade with the Kootenay by blocking the routes south and east. As a result, Thompson was forced to uncover a new route – one not yet under the scrutiny of the Blackfoot, which would allow free passage to and from the east. Once again, Thompson headed north.

THE ATHABASCA PASS

Thompson began this journey in December 1810, leading his group through the Athabasca Pass, where the temperature sank as low as minus 32 degrees Celsius. Shortages of food caused some of the men to desert when they reached the other side of the mountain pass, before the party reached the Columbia River. Thompson and his men set up camp to build a boat for themselves. They were unable to locate any birch trees from which to make a traditional bark canoe, so they used the wood of the large cedars around them, and tied the boards together with roots to make an eight-metre-long canoe.

Over the next few months the group travelled down the Columbia until it became clear to Thompson that this was indeed the river that continued on until it poured out into the Pacific. Gathering together a small group of men from his party, Thompson set off down the river in one final attempt to reach the sea.

They arrived at the mouth of the Columbia River, on the present-day Oregon/Washington border, on the 14th of July 1811, only to discover that another group of Europeans had made it there before them. John Jacob Astor's Pacific Fur Company had arrived and set up a trading post, which he named 'Astoria'. One of his men wrote about Thompson's arrival:

> *Toward midday we saw a large canoe*
> *with a flag displayed at her stern,*
> *rounding the point ... the flag she bore*
> *was British, and her crew was composed*
> *of eight Canadian boatmen or voyageurs.*
> *A well-dressed man, who appeared to*
> *be the commander, was the first to leap*
> *ashore.*

Thompson was enchanted by the sight of the ocean, but his travel-weary men didn't share his excitement. The first sighting of the ocean, he later wrote in his *Journal*, was:

> *to me ... a great pleasure, but my Men*
> *seemed disappointed; they had been*
> *accustomed to the boundless horizon*
> *of the great Lakes of Canada, and*
> *their high rolling waves; from the Ocean*
> *they expected a more boundless view,*
> *a something beyond the power of their*
> *senses which they could not describe.*

Two years later the North West Company purchased Astoria from the Pacific Fur Company, and at last they had their much-desired western outlet.

After a couple of weeks beside the ocean, Thompson decided to set off on the return journey, this time remaining on the Columbia River for the entire journey in order to map it properly. The journey back east proved just as difficult as his journey to the Pacific had been, but Thompson and his party finally crossed the Rockies and arrived in Montreal in the autumn of 1812. His long years of exploring in the north were over; he had travelled in the rivers, lakes and mountains of Canada and the northern United States for nearly 30 years, and it was time for a well-earned rest.

THOMPSON'S MAP

David Thompson retired from the North West Company at the age of 42, and moved his family to live in a town. During his retirement, he laboured long and hard to create a map

using the survey data he had meticulously recorded over the years. When he finished, he wrote in his memoir:

> *Thus I have fully completed the survey of this part of North America from sea to sea, and by almost innumerable astronomical Observations have determined the positions of the Mountains, Lakes and Rivers, and other remarkable places of the northern part of this Continent; the Maps of all of which have been drawn, and laid down in geographical position, being now the work of twenty seven years.*

His first map of the Canadian Northwest – from Hudson Bay to the Pacific – was hung in the Great Hall in Fort William. In 1814, it was replaced by an even larger one, some two by three metres. Thompson also created an atlas, but was unsuccessful in finding a publisher for it.

Thompson's map was undoubtedly his greatest achievement. It was so accurate that 100 years later it remained the basis for many of the maps issued by the Canadian government and the railway companies. He was even credited with the creation of the border that runs between Canada and the US today.

First Nations people gave Thompson the name Koo-Koo-Sint – which means 'Star-Gazer' – in recognition of his star-based mapwork. It wasn't that he was a starry-eyed dreamer, but rather a dedicated scientist using the best mapping technology of his day.

Despite Thompson's great successes, he died in extreme poverty and obscurity – forced even to pawn his surveying equipment and his overcoat to buy food for his family. But his legacy lives on through his surveys and his *Journals*, which produced some of the finest descriptions of the landscape and the people of the Canadian wilderness ever seen.

APPROACH FROM THE WEST

While Thompson and, before him, Mackenzie explored and then charted the Canadian West from Hudson's Bay to the Pacific Coast, exploration of another kind was taking place on the waters of the Pacific Ocean itself. If Thompson was considered by most to be the greatest land geographer of his time, then Captain James Cook was certainly the greatest charter of the seas, and he was responsible for mapping the Pacific coastline to open trade to the west.

Captain James Cook had a long and illustrious career. He was born in England in 1728, the son of a farm labourer. At the age of 18, he was hired as an apprentice by a ship owner in Whitby, where he learned to manoeuvre a variety of different craft. In 1755, he entered the Royal Navy as an able-bodied seaman. Two years later he became a 'master' and spent most of the Seven Years' War on the coast of the Atlantic provinces and the St Lawrence River. In 1758, he drafted his first map, of the Bay of Gaspe and the port, and collaborated on the 'New Chart of the River St Lawrence'.

In 1762, Cook was discharged from the Navy; however, five months later he was hired by the British Admiralty to undertake a detailed survey of the shores of Newfoundland, and identify territories specified under the 1763 Treaty of Paris. From 1766 to 1768, Cook developed a new model of hydrographic surveys combining trigonometric surveys made on land using a small craft to gather many soundings, information on aquatic fauna, coastal profiles and navigational notes.

CIRCUMNAVIGATING THE GLOBE

In 1768, Cook left for his first voyage around the globe, and his second lasted from 1772 to 1775. Upon his return to England, the Earl of Sandwich, First Lord of the Admiralty, called him 'the first navigator in Europe'. Elated by his success on the seas, Cook set himself the challenge of finding the Northwest Passage. He was aware that Samuel Hearne had got as far as the Arctic in 1771, and he'd also heard about the explorations of the Spaniard, Bartholomew de Font, on the west coast of the American continent. An added incentive was the English parliament's £20,000 reward, which would have provided him with enough money for life.

Cook needed no more convincing, and he set out for the Bering Strait in July 1776. Two years later, having travelled around the Cape of Good Hope and through New Zealand, Tahiti and the Sandwich Islands (now Hawaii), he reached the west coast of North America on the shores of Oregon. Violent winds pushed him northwest to Nootka Bay on Vancouver Island, which he believed to be the mainland. Here, he met with the Nootka people, who had already begun trading with Europeans.

After a short stay, he skirted the coast of Alaska, reaching the Bering Strait, and then heading northeast, where a wall of ice forced him to turn back. When he returned to the Sandwich Islands for the winter, he was assassinated there by a native of the islands, in Kealakekua Bay, in 1779. News of his tragic and shocking death reverberated around the world, but his work survived him, and his men were able to produce the hydrographic readings he had taken of the coast from Mount St Elias on the Alaskan-Canadian border, to the Bering Strait and beyond. The extent of the North American continent was now fully known, and its coastline waters meticulously charted.

In Europe, Cook was known primarily for his explorations of the Pacific; however, in Canada he became renowned primarily for the description he made of the coast of Vancouver Island. It is entirely fitting that the Englishman who carried on Cook's work, and provided the definitive 18th-century survey of the western Canadian coastline was George Vancouver, who had sailed with Cook on his second and third voyages.

It's important to note that Cook's last voyage was the prelude and in many ways the stimulus to long periods of international rivalry on the north-western Canadian coast. This rivalry, along with the arrival on the coast of the explorers, traders and settlers from the east, all played their part in the shaping of modern Canada.

GEORGE VANCOUVER

Born in 1747 at King's Lynn in Norfolk, George Vancouver entered the Royal Navy at the age of 14. Just a year later, he left for the southern continent on James Cook's ship, and was still there six years later when they arrived on the northwest coast of America. When Cook stopped at Nootka Bay for ship repairs and provisions, Vancouver was one of the first Europeans known to have landed on the island, and it was named in his honour.

After spending nearly a decade on war ships, mainly in the Caribbean, Vancouver was assigned to command an expedition to map out the west coast of America, and also to endeavour to find any navigable route that might eventually serve as a passage between the Pacific and the northwest Atlantic – in other words, the Northwest Passage.

A year after leaving England with two ships, in April 1791, Vancouver arrived on the west coast of North America, about 100 kilometres north of the city of San Francisco.

He travelled up and down this coast for the next three summers, undertaking hydrographic surveys and visiting inlets that could provide a possible passage. He was under orders to ignore any inlet or river 'further than it shall appear to be navigable by vessels of such burthen as might safely navigate the Pacific Ocean', and thus paid little attention to any streams or rivers that emptied into the sea.

Using small barks, which were not much larger than the traditional First Nations canoes, to conduct his surveys of the more indented areas of the shore, he attracted the attention of the native people, who were often tempted to raid them for arms and provisions. He did, however, build up some good relations with the indigenous people, and this was to stand him in good stead during his repeat visits to the shore.

In 1792, he had met Alcalá-Galiano and Valdés, two members of Malaspina's Spanish scientific expedition at anchor near the current city of Vancouver. Over the years, the explorers regularly exchanged information. In 1793, Vancouver explored the Dean Strait only a few weeks before

Alexander Mackenzie reached it by land. The following year, Vancouver ended his exploration in a bay of Baranof Island, in the Alexander Archipelago. In celebration of the end of his journey, he named the bay 'Port Conclusion', and began to head home.

Vancouver was, at that time, absolutely sure that the entrance to the Northwest Passage did not lie on the coastline that he had explored. His was one of the longest voyages of discovery in the 18th century, covering almost 100,000 kilometres in four years. Although he did not know it, he had been only a few kilometres away from the mouth of the passage, at the tip of the Alaskan coast.

Vancouver arrived back in England in 1795, whereupon he set about writing an account of his voyage. Just before its conclusion, he died in May 1798, at the age of 40, and his brother John completed the manuscript, which was published a few months later.

I stood on the same place that Vancouver stood, on the island that still bears his name. It's the westernmost tip of Canada, and from here I had a magnificent view of the coast and the incredible, varied wildlife. Many First Nations people still live here today, and, like Vancouver, and even Cook and Mackenzie before him, I am staggered by their extraordinary crafts, skills and traditions.

The province of British Columbia is home to 198 First Nations tribes – more than in any other territory in Canada. Getting to know some of them in person is a true honour, and they are able to recount their distinguished heritage vividly. To find out more about these people I am able to turn to the *Journals* kept by the great explorers who visited this land. Their words bring this beautiful part of the country alive, and were instrumental in passing on the traditions and beliefs of the people who lived here.

But the very best source of knowledge about these people and the land they inhabited came from a European who made it his home for almost three years – entirely against his will.

THE STORY OF JOHN JEWITT

One of the best descriptions of native life on the West Coast came from the pen of John R. Jewitt, who lived among the Nuu'chah'nulth (Nootka) people on Vancouver Island between 1803 and 1805. Jewitt was a 19-year-old English blacksmith employed aboard an American trading ship called *The Boston* when it sailed into Nootka Sound to trade with the native people.

Chief Maquinna boarded the ship to welcome them, and offered Captain Salter some fresh salmon. Jewitt, who had, at this point, had little contact with the native people, was astonished by the exchange, later writing: 'I had never before beheld a savage of any nation, it may readily be supposed that the novelty of their appearance, so different from any people that I had hitherto seen, excited in me strong feelings of surprise and curiosity.'

Maquinna was the chief of the Moachat group of the Nuu'chah'nulth, and Jewitt described him as being:

- - - - - - - - - - - - - - - - - - -

a man of dignified aspect, about six feet
tall in height and extremely straight and
well proportioned: his features were in
general good, and his face was rendered
remarkable by a large Roman nose, a
very uncommon form of feature among
these people; his complexion was of a
dark copper hue, though his face, legs,
and arms were on this occasion, so
covered with red paint, that their natural
colour could scarcely be perceived; his
eyebrows were painted black in two
broad stripes like a new moon, and his
long black hair, which shone with oil,
was fastened ... over with white down,
which gave him a most curious and
extraordinary appearance.

Maquinna was responsible for organising the trade for
his own village, and then taking goods on to other tribes,

returning native goods to the Europeans. His profits were remarkable, and he was a shrewd negotiator. Over two decades he had become a popular figure with the Europeans, who, in general, showed him great respect.

On this occasion, however, Maquinna was displeased to discover that a gun that had been offered to him by Captain Salter had a broken lock. When he returned it to the ship, Salter insulted the chief, and suggested that he had broken it himself. He gave the gun to Jewitt to repair, but carried on insulting Maquinna, who clearly understood what was being said.

Jewitt wrote: 'Unfortunately he understood but too well the meaning of the reproachful terms that the captain addressed him. He said not a word in reply, but his countenance sufficiently expressed the rage he felt though he exerted himself to suppress it.'

The following day Maquinna returned with several of his chiefs, but this time he wore a wooden mask that was carved as a fierce animal. The native people danced, and then stayed for dinner. While Jewitt was in the steerage cleaning muskets, he heard a commotion upstairs, and just avoided being decapitated by one of the chiefs who was wielding an axe. He fell to the floor, as the *Boston* was captured.

When he came to, Maquinna was standing over him, asking him a series of questions. Would he be Maquinna's slave for life? Fight for him in battle? Repair his muskets and make him knives?

Jewitt nodded his assent, and Maquinna recognised that the young blacksmith might indeed be useful. For this

reason, Jewitt's life was spared, and Maquinna led him to the quarterdeck where the 25 heads of the ship's captain and crew were arranged in a neat line. A second man, John Thompson, the ships' sail-maker, was found alive and subsequently spared when Jewitt convinced Maquinna that the older man was his father.

After emptying and then wrecking the *Boston*, the native people held a potlatch. A potlatch was a social occasion given by a host to establish or uphold his status in society. They were distinguished from mere 'feasts' in that guests were invited both to share food, and to receive gifts or payments. Potlatches were the place where ownership of economic and ceremonial privileges was asserted, displayed, and then formally transferred. It is a tradition that still exists today in the indigenous cultures of the northwest coast of Canada.

Maquinna invited 20 coastal tribes to join the feast of whale blubber, smoked herring spawn and dried fish. He transferred armloads of excess wealth including, as Jewitt noted, 'no less than one hundred muskets, the same number of looking glasses, four hundred yards of cloth and twenty casks of powder, besides other things'. It was the largest potlatch ever seen by most of the locals, and cemented even further Maquinna's superior position in the community.

After the massacre, Jewitt and Thompson were taken as slaves. While Thompson, an American, grew resentful of his keepers and was occasionally violent, Jewitt began to learn the language and get to know the people. He made fish hooks and knives for the chiefs in the tribe, and ornaments for the women and children. He became a popular slave, and therefore involved more fully in the daily lives of his captors than his fellow captive.

NOOTKA LIFE

Over the years, Jewitt noted every detail of Nootka life, describing in detail everything from clothing and weaponry to ceremonies and relationships and providing measurements for buildings and canoes. He observed the social interactions and found them, ultimately, not too distant from those of his own culture.

'In decorating their heads and faces they place their principal pride,' he wrote, 'and none of our most fashionable beaus, when preparing for a grand ball can be more particular: For I have known Maquinna after having been employed for more than an hour in painting his face, to rub the whole off and recommence the operation anew when it did not entirely please him.'

Although Maquinna could be a difficult master, holding himself in high esteem and being so strongly principled that he would rarely listen to reason, he grew close to Jewitt, taking him under his wing almost as if Jewitt were his own son. When he was in a good mood, Maquinna promised Jewitt that he would release him to the next trading boat that entered their waters; however, after word of the massacre had spread, no one came to trade there any more.

Almost two years after Jewitt's capture, Maquinna made the decision that Jewitt should be married to one of the local women and integrated into the trip. He magnanimously announced that if none of their own tribeswomen were favourable, they would travel to another tribe and purchase a bride for the young man. Although this prospect filled Jewitt with horror, he wrote: 'Reduced to this sad extremity, with death on the one side, and matrimony on the other, I thought proper to choose what appeared to me the least of the two evils, and consent to be married.'

And so it was that Jewitt, Maquinna and 50 of the tribesmen loaded two canoes with offerings, such as muskets, cloths and sea-otter pelts, and set out meet the women of the A-i-tiz-zart tribe. After a feast of herring spawn and whale oil, Jewitt chose the 17-year-old daughter of the chief as his bride. His new wife Eu-stoch-ee-exqua was beautiful and gentle, but Jewitt was uncomfortable with the whole affair. He became even more so when it became clear that Maquinna planned to use his 'marriage' as the first step towards his full integration in the tribe. He was forced to paint himself in red and black like the other tribesmen, and wear a breech cloth instead of his European garments. However, he continued to retreat to the forest on

Sundays to pray to his Christian God, thus holding on to the last remnants of both his faith and his own culture.

Jewitt grew melancholy, and Maquinna agreed that his wife should be returned to her tribe until he was able to shift his depression and care for her properly. Surprisingly, Eu-stoch-ee-exqua begged to stay, and promised to nurse him back to health. Jewitt later wrote:

> *I told her she must go, for that I did*
> *not think I should ever recover, which*
> *in truth I but little expected, and that*
> *her father would take good care of her*
> *... I was greatly affected with the simple*
> *expressions of her regard for me, and*

could not but feel strongly interested for
this poor girl, who in all her conduct
towards me, had discovered so much
mildness and attention to my wishes;
and had it not been that I considered her
as an almost insuperable obstacle to my
being permitted to leave the country,
I should no doubt have felt the
deprivation of her society a real loss.

JEWITT'S RELEASE

Jewitt had been with the Nuu'chah'nulth for almost three years when, in 1805, his fortunes changed. He wrote, 'On the morning of the nineteenth of July, a day that will be ever held by me in grateful remembrance, of the mercies of God ... my ears were saluted with the joyful sound of three cannon, and the cries of the inhabitants, exclaiming ... strangers – white men.'

Samuel Hill was captain of the *Lydia*, a trading ship from Boston, which had been anchored in the sound. He had heard of Jewitt and Thompson's plight, as a result of the letters that Jewitt had sent from time to time with other chiefs who had visited the tribe to trade. Bursting with excitement at the prospect of being released, Jewitt nonetheless feigned lack of interest in order to avoid rousing the suspicions of his captors.

Some of the chiefs shouted that the two men should be killed; others thought they should be taken deep into the forest until the ship left the sound. Jewitt and Thompson were waiting to hear their fate when suddenly Maquinna decided that he would go onboard the ship to assess the trading potential. He asked Jewitt to write him a letter of reference, saying that he and Thompson had been well cared for during their stay with the tribe. Jewitt wrote the following:

> *Dear Sir,*
> *The bearer of this letter is the Indian*
> *king by the name of Maquinna. He*

was the instigator of the capture of
the ship Boston, of Boston in North
America, John Salter captain, and of the
murder of twenty-five men of her crew,
the two only survivors being now on shore
— Wherefore I hope you will take care
to confine him according to his merits,
putting him in your dead lights, and
keeping so good a watch over him, that he
cannot escape from you. By so doing we
shall be able to obtain our release in the
course of a few hours.

Maquinna happily carried the letter on board, where he was arrested. The canoe soon returned to land without the chief, and the native people were outraged by Jewitt's betrayal. They alternately begged and threatened him to do something to ensure the release of Maquinna, and so Jewitt agreed to go aboard the ship. With his long hair piled on his head and held by a twig, his red and black face and body paint, and his bearskin wrap, Captain Samuel Hill later wrote that he had never in his life seen any human in so wild a state. Jewitt spent the night in a cabin with Maquinna, who was in irons, and who tried to convince Jewitt to secure his release.

The following morning Jewitt returned to the shore, gathered together the remaining cargo from the *Boston*, and arranged for a final trade – the chief for the goods. Maquinna left the ship in good spirits, promising future trade with the captain. Then, as Jewitt wrote,

> *grasping both my hands with much*
> *emotion, while the tears trickled down his*
> *cheeks, he bade me farewell, and stept*
> *into the canoe, which immediately paddled*
> *him on shore … Notwithstanding my*
> *joy at my deliverance, I could not avoid*
> *experiencing a painful sensation on*
> *parting with this savage chief, who had*
> *preserved my life, and in general treated*

me with kindness, and considering their
ideas and manners, much better than
could have been expected.

Jewitt and Thompson did not arrive back in Boston until 1807, five full years after leaving England for an exciting new land. Jewitt left behind his five-month-old son with Eu-stoch-ee-exqua, who Maquinna promised to retrieve and raise as his own. He later married a white woman, with whom he had five children, and settled in Connecticut. When he published his diary, it received critical admiration and some fairly good sales. Jewitt died at the age of 37, in 1821. Maquinna was last seen in 1825 by a Hudson's Bay trader, who described the peculiar sight of the elderly chief shuffling on board the trading ships, anxious to strike a deal.

This is, to me, a fascinating and compelling story that provides real insight into the character of the First Nations men and women. I can think of no other story that so closely and accurately documents the relationship between the native people and the Europeans, and the intricate details of the native culture. I set out to explore the north-western territory using Jewitt's notes as my guide.

THE PACIFIC COAST

Like the many explorers before me, and Jewitt himself, I could not fail to notice the amazing red cedar trees lining the coastal regions, which were used not only for the First Nations dugout canoes, but also for their incredible totem poles.

For First Nations people in the northwest, totem poles serve to proclaim a clan's status. The figures (known as 'crests') carved onto the poles symbolise a clan's mythological history, as well as the rights and privileges it enjoys. Although totem poles had been made long before the arrival of the Europeans in the late 18th century, they became increasingly popular. The fur trade made many of the First Nations very wealthy (as in the case of Maquinna), and encouraged greater displays of privilege and rank.

Greater access to metal tools also allowed the artists to carve the cedar more quickly, and with more precision. Although pole production began to decline in the 20th century, they continue to be made today as a universal emblem of the First Nations cultures.

I met Gisele Martin, a First Nation woman with great knowledge of traditional crafts and skills. She explained to me the meanings of symbols on her family totem poles, and how the intricate carvings of birds and animals represented aspects of personality and character. For example, a wolf denoted intelligence, leadership and a strong sense of family, while a Thunderbird with closed wings was carved

in memory of an aunt who had died. The eagle represented great strength and prestige, and the raven denoted creation and knowledge, as the bringer of light.

I also visited the site of the world's tallest totem pole, at Alert Bay. At 52 metres (in two parts), it was carved by six Kwakwaka'wakw artists. The fourteen figures depicted on this pole represent some of the tribes of the Kwakwaka'wakw nation, and some of its makers are still around today, still keeping the old traditions alive.

I was fascinated to visit the Alert Bay Museum, which has examples of totem poles and all kinds of local carvings as well as basketwork, ship models and an archive of photographs showing life in the area over the last century. There is a strong desire to keep the old traditions going, particularly amongst the Kwakwaka'wakw, and they still hold ceremonial potlatches, at which there are speeches, singing and dancing, and gifts are distributed by the host family. I was amazed to find that Jewitt's account of the potlatch was not only accurate in the detail, but also sympathetic to the sentiment behind these unique events.

Potlatches were banned for several decades from 1855, as part of a government drive to appease the missionaries, who believed it was an 'obstacle' to 'civilising natives'. Its formal return to acceptability was widely celebrated on the Pacific Coast, and it is now very important to the Kwakwaka'wakw people. They give regular talks in schools to try and make sure that the traditions are passed on to the next generation.

I was reluctant to leave Alert Bay, so well preserved were the memories and heritage of this unique place and its culture, skills and beliefs. It is people like these who keep the flames of history alive and burning, and Canada would be a much poorer country without them.

MEARES ISLAND

My time in the northwest was drawing to a close, but I could not leave her beautiful shores without paying a visit to Meares Island. It is named after John Meares (1756–1809),

unfortunately no relation to me but an Irish navigator and explorer who played a role in establishing Britain's claims to the northwest coast of America.

Meares Island is one of the many islands surrounding the town of Tofino, and it is located in the Clayoquot Sound region. Home to the main village of the Tla-o-aui-aht First Nations, it was also the site of Fort Defiance, an American fur-trading post that was founded by a trader called Captain Robert Gray in 1791. It is now a popular tourist attraction, not only because it is a haven of First Nations culture, but also because it hosts some of the tallest trees in British Columbia. Some of the red cedar trees here reach 50 metres in height, with a circumference of more than 20 metres. I was staggered by the multitude of uses that the native people found for the trees, using them to create homes, boats, weapons, the ubiquitous totem poles, masks and other ceremonial wear, as well as in artwork. I was also privileged to watch a master craftsman at work here, as Gisele Martin showed me some of her cedar weavings.

Many of the skills that I use in my own work are only practised today because of the diligent care that the explorers and the First Nations took to preserve them. By following in their footsteps I had learned more about the land than I ever thought possible at the outset.

But despite their often heroic efforts, Cook, Vancouver, Mackenzie and Thompson failed in their attempts to discover the fabled Northwest Passage, and thus always felt a niggling sense of disappointment and even failure that this challenge had eluded them. Some people were even beginning to suggest that such a passage simply did not exist. Maybe it genuinely wasn't possible to cross from the Atlantic to the Pacific via the waterways of the northwest. Following in the footsteps of Samuel Hearne, an explorer called Dr John Rae set out to prove the sceptics wrong.

CHAPTER 6

FOLLOWING IN HEARNE'S FOOTSTEPS

The trails blazed by Samuel Hearne in the mid-18th century set the template for a number of other explorers who ventured deep into the Canadian forests, across the towering mountain ranges, and into the bleak north. Each had very different aims, but, like Hearne, they chose to journey in the manner of the local inhabitants of the land, and accrue and utilise the native skills and knowledge that would allow them to explore and survive in the hostile wilderness. As a result, their names are every bit as important as Hearne's, and their successes just as much a part of the history and development of Canada. Mackenzie and Thompson's ultimate goal was to identify and chart the Northwest Passage but in the end they failed. Several decades after them, another Hearne follower, Dr John Rae, set out to see if he could establish its whereabouts.

As the fur trade expanded throughout the land owned by the Hudson's Bay Company and beyond, exploration was not just encouraged but essential. Apart from the commercial implications of ensuring that trading posts were available to hunters across the territory, there was also a competitive spirit between the companies that monopolised the trade. Each wanted to be first to explore and map uncharted land, and to achieve this, they encouraged a handful of their finest young men to learn the skills necessary to follow in the footsteps of Samuel Hearne. In my opinion Hearne's travels would remain the standard for other explorers for decades to come.

One of these explorers was Dr John Rae, and he would go on to succeed where so many others had failed. For Rae was the man who would eventually find the missing link in the holy grail of 18th- and 19th-century exploration – Canada's

Northwest Passage. Hearne had discounted the presence of this passage in the Coppermine area, having travelled to Inuit territory in the northwest of the country, and seen nothing that excited his interest.

Among countless others, seasoned explorers Mackenzie, Thompson, Cook and Vancouver also failed to find it. But the long-held belief that this passage existed continued to spur on explorers, and inspired extensive sponsorship by the fur companies – and, indeed, whole nations. Sadly, its eventual discovery was enshrouded with controversy, and the humble man who charted it was vilified through circumstances completely beyond his control.

AN UNSUNG HERO

John Rae was a humble man, and known to his contemporaries for his modest and unassuming manner. His is a fascinating, but equally frustrating and sad story, and his achievements have often been overlooked in the maelstrom

of misinformation and defamation that surrounded one of
his expeditions.

He remains one of my favourite explorers not just because
of the dignified way in which he pursued his activities, but
also because of the respectful manner in which he integrated
the knowledge of the local people, and adjusted his ways to
live in harmony with his environment. Like Samuel Hearne
before him, he was able to survive and venture deep into
the northern wilderness because he adopted the skills of

the First Nations, and used their understanding of the world around them as his guide.

John Rae is undoubtedly one of Orkney's greatest heroes. His memorial is prominent in St Magnus Cathedral, which towers over the town of Kirkwall in the Orkney Isles. Rae was born in September 1813, at the Hall o' Clestrain in Orphir. He was the son of a factor of Sir William Honeyman's Orkney estate, and his father was able to bring up his family in some comfort, in affluent surroundings.

From an early age, John Rae was an outdoorsman, making the most of his rural location to acquire some of the skills that would make his later exploits so successful. He learned to sail, climb, trek, hunt and fish, and when his father was made the Orkney agent of the Hudson's Bay Company, he would accompany him on the short sea crossing between Clestrain and Stromness, where the HBC had its offices. Here, the young man would watch the company's many supply ships stocking up at Login's Well before setting off across the Atlantic.

THE TRAVELLING SURGEON

By 1833, John Rae had qualified as a surgeon in Edinburgh, and was keen to make the most of his skills. He signed on as a surgeon aboard the HBC ship *Prince of Wales*, whose destination was Moose Factory in James Bay, at the southern end of Canada's Hudson Bay. He initially planned to spend a single season in the new world, but the early arrival of winter forced him to remain on the desolate Charlton Island, and despite the harsh conditions, he became enthralled by what he described as 'the wild sort of life to be found in the Hudson's Bay Company service'. It took little deliberation on his part to accept the post of surgeon at Moose Factory, and there he remained for the next decade.

His work involved tending to both the European and the Indian employees of the company and he travelled between them with an open mind. In the bitter cold of the Canadian winter, the only way for Rae to reach his patients was by snowshoe. Like so many other things in his life, he quickly mastered the technique. There are stories of him walking half the night, through deep snow, just to catch up with the postman because he'd forgotten to post a letter. He eventually became so proficient that he designed his own style of snowshoes to tackle the variety of environments and conditions he endured. Local legend has it that Rae was the best snow-walker of his time. In fact, over two months between 1844 and 1845, he covered almost 2,000 kilometres on foot. The Inuit gave him the name *Aglooka*, meaning 'he who takes long strides'.

Rae was a natural student, and absorbed the way of life of the area around him. He regarded himself as a student of the native Cree, and from them he learned essential skills that he would practise and then master until he was as adept as any First Nations people. He was taught how to make and maintain snowshoes, and how to hunt for caribou and store the meat. Later on he learned from the Inuit how to ice the runners of a sled, combat snow-blindness and construct a shelter. In a nutshell, John Rae learned the skills he would need to survive even the harshest elements.

He also developed friendships with the native people, who were honoured by his great respect for their culture, traditions and skills. Eventually, he became widely regarded as the leading authority on First Nations methods of Arctic survival and travel.

Although many of his contemporaries frowned upon his insistence on spending so much time with the 'natives' – even dressing like them for practical purposes – his activities and knowledge soon attracted the interest of those at the helm of the HBC. His strength, self-reliance and clarity of purpose commanded attention, and in 1845, John Rae was chosen by Hudson's Bay Company Governor Sir George Simpson to lead an expedition to search for the Northwest Passage, and fill in the last blanks on the maps of the northern coast.

After some time spent in Toronto studying surveying, Rae left York Factory in June 1846 with 10 men and two seven-metre boats. John Rae was headed for the Arctic.

INTO THE ARCTIC

Canada's Arctic coast was becoming an obsession for Britain. The discovery of a route across the top of Canada could revolutionise sea trade to the Far East, offering the prospect of an alternative to the otherwise progressively hazardous journey through French and Spanish waters. Britain was becoming increasingly desperate to win the race to find the passage, but despite the extraordinarily generous reward of £20,000 no one had yet managed to discover it.

Thanks to the work of many brave explorers, much of the route had been mapped by the mid-19th century; however, attempts to complete the passage had been stymied by huge tracts of immovable sea ice. No one in the HBC's history had been able to negotiate the frozen sea, but this time they believed they'd found their man. John Rae's expedition was the first Arctic overland attempt to complete the route and find the missing link, and he was undoubtedly the man for the job.

Although many travellers, including Hearne himself, had approached the Arctic mainland, it remained uncharted and was still an unknown entity. Rae and his men were the first Europeans ever to spend a winter there, and their survey of the blanks on the map brought them to a place they called Pelly Bay. Rae's party travelled on foot, hauling a sledge through the almost impenetrable snow. Like Hearne before him, he adopted the ideology of the native people, choosing to live off the land rather than dragging heavy loads of provisions. He carried a meagre quantity of supplies, despite his intention to stay for over a year. His men were dumbfounded, but accepted that his was a superior knowledge, made evident by the considerable skill he showed in negotiating both the elements and the landscape.

In this part of the world, surprisingly little has changed since Rae first set foot here. Many First Nations people still rely on their traditional skills, and as recently as the 1960s, their way of life had changed only imperceptibly from that encountered by Rae. He understood their dependence upon the caribou population, and was already familiar with the skills necessary to hunt them, and preserve their meat. He became adept at wielding the *kakuvak* spear, just as Hearne did. Knowing how to find food here all year round was crucial to Rae's expeditions, and it is doubtful that any other explorer could have embraced and implemented this knowledge more than he did.

That's not to say that he didn't make a few mistakes en route. When Rae first arrived in the Arctic, he built a traditional Scottish hut from stone, but it was the wrong

technology in the wrong place. There were days when the cold was so fierce that he and his men were unable even to venture out of bed. When Rae realised his error, he quickly made it his business to learn how to build an igloo, which used the ice and snow as a natural source of insulation. Piece by piece he acquired the skills needed for life this far north – and an ideology that would ensure his survival.

Today there is a permanent settlement at Pelly Bay, now known as Kugaaruk, a thriving community in which First Nations people make it their business to ensure that traditional skills and knowledge continue through the generations. Once a week, elders visit the schools to impress upon the children the importance of their heritage, and teach them the skills that made the survival of their people possible. My travels there gave me a glimpse of the kind of people and lifestyles Rae would have come across.

In April 1847, the expedition crossed Rae Isthmus to reach Lord Mayor's Bay, mapping the shore of the Simpson Peninsula on the return journey. Rae and his men then explored the west coast of Melville Peninsula, with the two legs of the journey adding up to over 1,000 kilometres of new coastline mapped. When he had completed his expedition, Rae had not yet found the passage, but the blank spaces on the map were getting smaller and smaller.

Eager to build on Rae's success, and impatient to find the passage before the HBC could, the British Navy commissioned their own expedition by sea, and decided it would be led by the inimitable Sir John Franklin.

THE TRAGEDY OF
SIR JOHN FRANKLIN

Sir John Franklin was an officer in the Royal Navy and an Arctic explorer who was born in Lincolnshire in 1786. He joined the Navy at the age of 12, and became a Navy careerman. Although he took part in the Battle of Trafalgar, he is best remembered for his surveys of the Arctic, during which he created maps of almost 5,000 kilometres of northern Canada's coastline.

Altogether, Franklin made four journeys to the Arctic, the last three as commanding officer. In 1819, he left on his second expedition to explore the coast of the Arctic Ocean eastwards, starting at the Coppermine River. To get there, he acquired an HBC ship. He landed at York Factory, and passed through Cumberland House, and then on through Fort Chipewyan, a NWC post in what is now the province of Alberta. Although he did recruit native guides and hunters, the ongoing conflict between the two fur companies made it difficult to secure labour. Nonetheless, he got as far as Winter Lake in the summer of 1820, and he went on to spend the winter there.

By the time that Franklin reached this place, which he called 'Fort Enterprise', he and his men had realised that their provisions were inadequate, and even though more were supplied at Fort Chipewyan, they did not last the journey. By the time they reached the mouth of the Coppermine River in 1821, Franklin and his men were starving and forced to eat the leather on their shoes and clothing. (It's interesting to remember that both Hearne and Rae had reached this point without eating their footwear.) Nine men were lost on the journey and Franklin was deeply upset by the experience. When he returned to England in 1822, he found a public eager to know the details of his horrific journey, and he became a national hero.

Buoyed up by public interest, he agreed to undertake a third expedition, before which he took care to acquire huge stores of provisions, and a number of watercraft that had been built for the journey. He left Great Bear River in June 1826. Franklin went half of the way to his planned destination at Icy Cape before deciding to return because of the cold. However, my experience of the north leads me to question some of Franklin's writing:

> *Many of them had their legs*
> *swelled and inflamed from continually*
> *wading in ice-cold water while launching*
> *the boats, not only when we accidentally*
> *ran on shore, but every time that*
> *it was requisite to embark, or to land*

*upon this shallow coast. Nor were these
symptoms to be overlooked in coming
to a determination; for though no one
who knows the resolute disposition of
British sailors can be surprised at their
more than readiness to proceed, I felt
that it was my business to judge of their
capability of so doing, and not to allow
myself to be seduced by their ardour,
however honourable to them, and cheering
to me.*

Despite being cut short, this expedition was fruitful, and during his travels Franklin not only mapped almost 2,000 kilometres of coastline, but also managed to collect information on geology and weather, as well as making notes on 663 plants. In 1827, Franklin published the accounts of his voyage, for which he was rewarded, among other things, with a knighthood in 1829.

In 1845, at the age of 59, John Franklin offered to give

up his comfortable retirement of some 20 years in order to lead another expedition to the Artic to search for the Northwest Passage once again. He took two ships – the *Erebus* and the *Terror*. The front of each ship was set with sheets of iron to enable them to push their way through the ice, and although they were whaling ships, they were also fitted with small steam engines and a propeller. Each ship carried enough coal for 12 days, and the engines would be used only when it was necessary to break the ice.

His crew was comprised of 129 officers and men from the Royal Navy, and they brought with them provisions to last three years. Food, clothing, tobacco, rum, over 2,000 books, and some 8,000 tins of food were stowed in the ships, which set sail from Greenhithe in Kent, on 19th May 1845. On 26th July, the captain of a whaling ship saw them off the coast of Baffin Island. This is the last time the ships or men were ever seen. They didn't return from the voyage and no word was received from them.

In 1848, Sir John Richardson, a Scottish surgeon, naturalist and explorer who had travelled in the Arctic with

Franklin back in the 1920s, determined to set out and find him, and John Rae of the Hudson's Bay Company was his natural choice to be second-in-command.

THE DOWNFALL OF JOHN RAE

Following his expedition earlier that year, Dr John Rae had become something of a local legend, and his navigation and survival skills were renowned. Although he was keen to continue his own search for the Northwest Passage, he leapt at the opportunity to work under Richardson, who was particularly renowned for his descriptions of the natural history of the Arctic. And he was right to do so, for on his travels with Richardson, Rae was able to chart many more territories of the northern Canadian coast and get further towards his ultimate goal.

Richardson and Rae left Sault Ste Marie on 4th May 1848, and in one of the fastest canoe expeditions in history, they reached the mouth of the Mackenzie River on 3rd August.

Turning east, they searched the coast as far as the mouth of Coppermine River, finding no trace of Franklin and his men.

Richardson returned home, but Rae attempted another summer of searching. However, ice conditions prevented him from crossing to Victoria Island, and when his Eskimo interpreter drowned at Bloody Falls (the only fatality on any of his expeditions), Rae returned home as well.

In 1851, Rae set out on a third expedition, this time on foot with two men, two sledges and five dogs. They explored over 1,000 kilometres of Victoria Island's coastline — by sea and on foot. Unknown to Rae, his return journey took him to within 80 kilometres of Franklin's ships, which were trapped in the ice to the east. He wouldn't find that out for another three years, though.

Rae's fourth and last expedition took place in 1853, and was actually undertaken to complete his survey of the continental coastline for the HBC, but when he reached Pelly Bay, the Inuit gave him second-hand news of the Franklin expedition's fate. Seemingly some Inuit had seen dead and dying men some four years earlier and it sounded as though it could be them. Rae moved on to map still more coastline along the west side of Boothia Peninsula, and that's when he made the crucial discovery that King William Land was in fact an island and that the stretch of water separating it from the mainland, now known as Rae Strait, was the missing link in the Northwest Passage. Rae couldn't navigate through the frozen Strait – it wasn't until 1903–6 that Roald Amundsen made it through the ice – but Rae had completed his life's quest and found a way through from the Atlantic to the Pacific to the north of Canada. His joy, however, was to be tempered, and his success completely overshadowed, by the events that followed.

On his return journey, Rae stopped at Repulse Bay. Here, the Inuit brought him a silver plate, a medal and several pieces of cutlery with the names or initials of Franklin and his officers. After many sessions of intensive questioning and cross-examination that lasted over two months, Rae uncovered the truth of Franklin's fate.

According to the native accounts, ice had crushed their ships and the last remaining men had perished in the winter of 1850. Many of the search parties had come tantalisingly close to finding them, but their efforts were now known to be completely in vain. Rae then learned that the Inuit had discovered some 30 bodies and a number of graves and it seemed most of the men had died of starvation. None of the men had any significant survival skills and it was discovered later that they had been poisoned by lead contained in their tinned provisions, which made their food supplies largely inedible. They were completely unable to live off the land, which, although barren and cold, could have supported them if they'd had the requisite knowledge.

Rae wrote: 'Some of the bodies had been buried (probably those of the first victims of famine); some were in a tent or tents; others under the boat, which had been turned over to form a shelter, and several lay scattered about in different directions.' He added, 'From the mutilated state of many of the bodies and the contents of the kettles, it is evident that our wretched Countrymen had been driven to the last dread alternative – cannibalism – as a means of prolonging existence.'

And from here on, things began to go very wrong for Dr John Rae. Because he had experienced such positive relationships with the natives, and grew to trust their honesty, he did not doubt the fact that they were telling him the truth. For this reason, and because winter was approaching, Rae did not actually visit the site, choosing instead to take the unhappy news back to England.

LADY FRANKLIN'S FURY

Bringing with him the physical evidence that the Inuit had supplied to back up their story, Rae presented his conclusions to Franklin's widow, Lady Jane Franklin, and the Royal Navy. His conclusions were immediately condemned and his integrity was questioned. Lady Franklin refused to accept Rae's findings and mounted a sustained attack on him. Since her husband's disappearance, she had determinedly worked to establish him as a courageous explorer, who had bravely sought and discovered the Northwest Passage. She felt that Rae's discoveries not only cast shame upon her husband, but also stripped him of the glory of being the first to uncover the passage – which, of course, he never was.

It became a *cause célèbre* – and society sided with the Franklins. Leaping to Lady Franklin's aid was none other than Charles Dickens, who published a series of articles rejecting Rae's conclusions and the unorthodox means by which he had reached them. He, along with Lady Franklin, refused to accept that any member of the Navy 'would or could in any extremity of hunger, alleviate that pains of starvation by this horrible means'.

To his credit, Rae refused to retract his conclusions and throughout the furious attacks on his character, he stood by his report into the disappearance. Eventually an expedition was sent to the site by Lady Franklin. Here, a message left by a Lieutenant Crozier, second in command was discovered. It confirmed that Sir John Franklin had died on the 11th of June 1847 – the 25th man to perish on the journey.

Skeletons of some of the last survivors were found in the

cairn in 1859, and they appeared to confirm that the men had, indeed, resorted to cannibalism, although Lady Franklin and her supporters would maintain that they must have been eaten by 'natives' – or by polar bears.

Dr John Rae never lived down the ignominy of his discovery, and the vitriol of Lady Franklin and her influential friends all but wiped his achievements from their rightful place in history. He was given the reward that had been offered by the British Admiralty, and he duly shared this among his men, but he received no positive recognition for either his discovery of the Northwest Passage or the fate of the Franklin Expedition. John Rae retired from the Hudson's Bay Company in 1856 at the age of 43 but, unbowed, he refused to let the events crush his great love of exploration, and it was not long before he set off again.

In 1857, Rae moved to the south, to what is now Hamilton, Ontario, where he practised as a surgeon. In 1860, he married Kate Thompson in Toronto, and then returned to England. That year, he surveyed for the Atlantic Telegraph, via the Faroe Islands, Iceland and Greenland. And in 1884, he accepted a position that brought him back into the service of the Hudson's Bay Company. The HBC, in partnership with the Western Telegraph Union Company, were busy exploring the possibility of creating a telegraph route through Siberia, the Bering Strait, Alaska and British Columbia. Rae was asked to survey a section of the proposed route from Red River to Victoria.

Once again he was back in the country that he loved, and he was able to survey a considerable stretch of the Fraser River in a dugout canoe, and without a guide. His survey notes were later used in the development of the Canadian West.

Rae then returned with his wife to his native Orkney Isles, eventually retiring to London. He wrote a book and 20 papers, and had 45 letters published in *Nature* magazine. But because of the still-acrimonious climate surrounding his Arctic activities, his correspondence from this period, edited by E. E. Rich, would not be published until 1953.

Rae died in London on the 22nd of July 1893, and was interred in the churchyard of St Magnus Cathedral. His wife, who was childless, lived until 1919.

Although they had failed to find the Northwest Passage, Franklin and his officers were posthumously knighted. Rae, on the other hand, was the only major explorer of the era not to receive a knighthood. Quite apart from his other significant achievements, Rae had found the Northwest Passage that had been sought for so many centuries, but he received no recognition or award.

But John Rae's achievements will go down in history as one of the most important of his time. His intelligence, accurate observations, competent writing and accomplished medical skills comprised just a small proportion of the characteristics that made him such a great man. He was, by all accounts, humble and kind – a gentle, pleasant and frugal man, who quietly respected the choices and the lives of the people around him.

He drew great pleasure from continuing to learn new skills and acquire new knowledge throughout his lifetime, and he made extraordinary use of the wisdom and traditions of the peoples who populated the vast country he came to call home. He was adventurous yet methodical, intrepid but never arrogant. John Rae paid tribute to his native teachers not just by living the way they did, and crediting them with much of his success, but also by helping to ensure that their culture and traditions were carried into the new age. And he was honest enough to forfeit a richly deserved knighthood because he stood by his honour, and that of his Inuit friends.

If Samuel Hearne was responsible for taking the first steps to open up the Canadian north, it was most surely Dr John Rae who completed that mission. The Northwest Passage was the holy grail of all exploration, and Rae quietly set about finding it, in the company of the people who had made it their home. His achievements may not have received the recognition they deserved, but his legacy will live on in the bleak, windswept north of Canada, where his work helped to found a nation.

The geography of this still-wild country is both absorbing and challenging, and on my travels I have seen breathtaking sights, and experienced many inexplicably moving moments. From the deepest reaches of the boreal

forest, the remote trading posts and the stunning heights of the Rocky Mountains to the rushing waters of the inland rivers and the frozen north, the Northern wilderness is alive with legend, and replete with history and adventure. I can almost hear the voices of the men who defined the borders of Canada, and opened it up to the modern world. And while they may remain unsung heroes in the annals of history, their legacy, their unremittingly hard and dangerous work, is here for all to see.

This is a country built on trade, and developed by a huge company. Enterprise, commercial interests and even greed may have provided the impetus for the great explorers to be funded and directed across this vast country, but each of these men was true to himself, and applied the most staggeringly sophisticated skills and knowledge to explore and chart a land that covers such a huge proportion of the globe.

In places this remains a barren land – inhospitable and bitterly cold, year round – but at the same time it is teeming with bounty, in nature and in the cultures of the people who inhabit it. With every step of my journey I came across another story carved into the landscape, and I love the fact that those stories will remain there, now, forever.

INDEX

ACKNOWLEDGEMENTS

Thanks as always to my TV crew: Ben Southwell, Julia Foot, Sally Dyas, Cassy Walkling, Jo Fletcher, Nicole Kruysse, Barrie Foster, Alan Duxbury, Tim Green, Andy Morton, Ross Neasham, Sue Loder and Pete Lawrence.

Thank you to Rupert, Laura, Humphrey, Gill, Ned, and everyone at Hodder who helped to put this book together.

And a special thank you to everyone who assisted us out in Canada:

Alex Strachan, Allan Main, Allen Niptanatiak, Andy Korsos, the Archives of Manitoba, everyone at the Canadian Canoe Museum, the Canadian Rangers, Carol James, Chief Adam Dick, David Malaher, Dennis Compayre, Don Willson, Fort Carlton, Gisele Martin, Grant Newman, the Hudson's Bay Company, Ila Bussidor, J David Henry, Janette Park, Jean and Ivan Craigie, Jeremy Ward, Joan Murray, Joe Martin, Ken Lister, Kevin Callan, Kim Recalma-Clutesi, Lavern Thompson, Leanne Playter, Nancy Turner, the Natural History Museum, Norman Dokis, Nunavut Parks, Parks Canada, the people of Kugaaruk, Pinock Smith, Ross Macdonald, the Royal Ontario Museum, Sally Milne, Scott Adams, Scott Whiting, the staff of Prince Albert National Park, the Tlicho people of Rae Edzo, Tom Andrews and Tom Charles

PICTURE CREDITS

All photography is by Ray Mears.

Paul Kane sketches are from his sketchbook, courtesy of the Royal Ontario Museum.

Map on contents page: courtesy of Hudson's Bay Company Archives/Archives of Manitoba (HBCA library RB FC 3212.2 H4 frontispiece)

Portrait of Samuel Hearne in colour section 3, page 2: courtesy of Hudson's Bay Company Archives/Archives of Manitoba (HBCA Documentary Art, P-167)